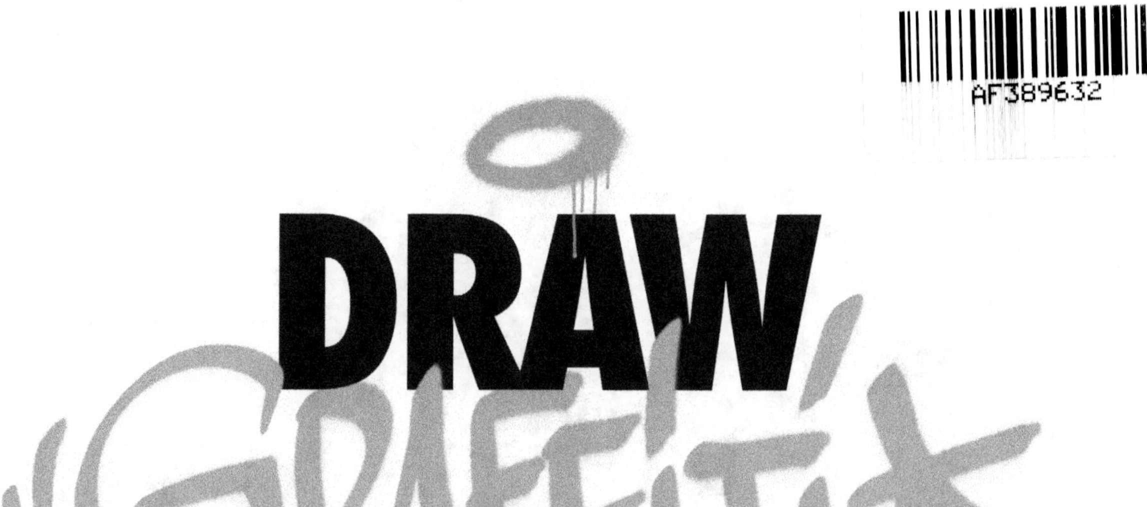

Draw Graffiti - A Beginners Guide To Graffiti Letters
First published in 2022 by Graffiti Bible
Contact@graffitibible.com

The information and opinions in this book are provided for information purposes only. They are not intended to constitute legal or other professional advice, and should not be relied upon as such. Any activity discribed in this book should be carried out legally. The publisher does not encourage readers to engage in illegal activity in the real world.

ISBN 978-87-998628-9-4

 @TheRealGraffitibible

 @Graffitibible

 @Graffitibible

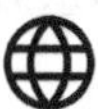 Graffitibible.com

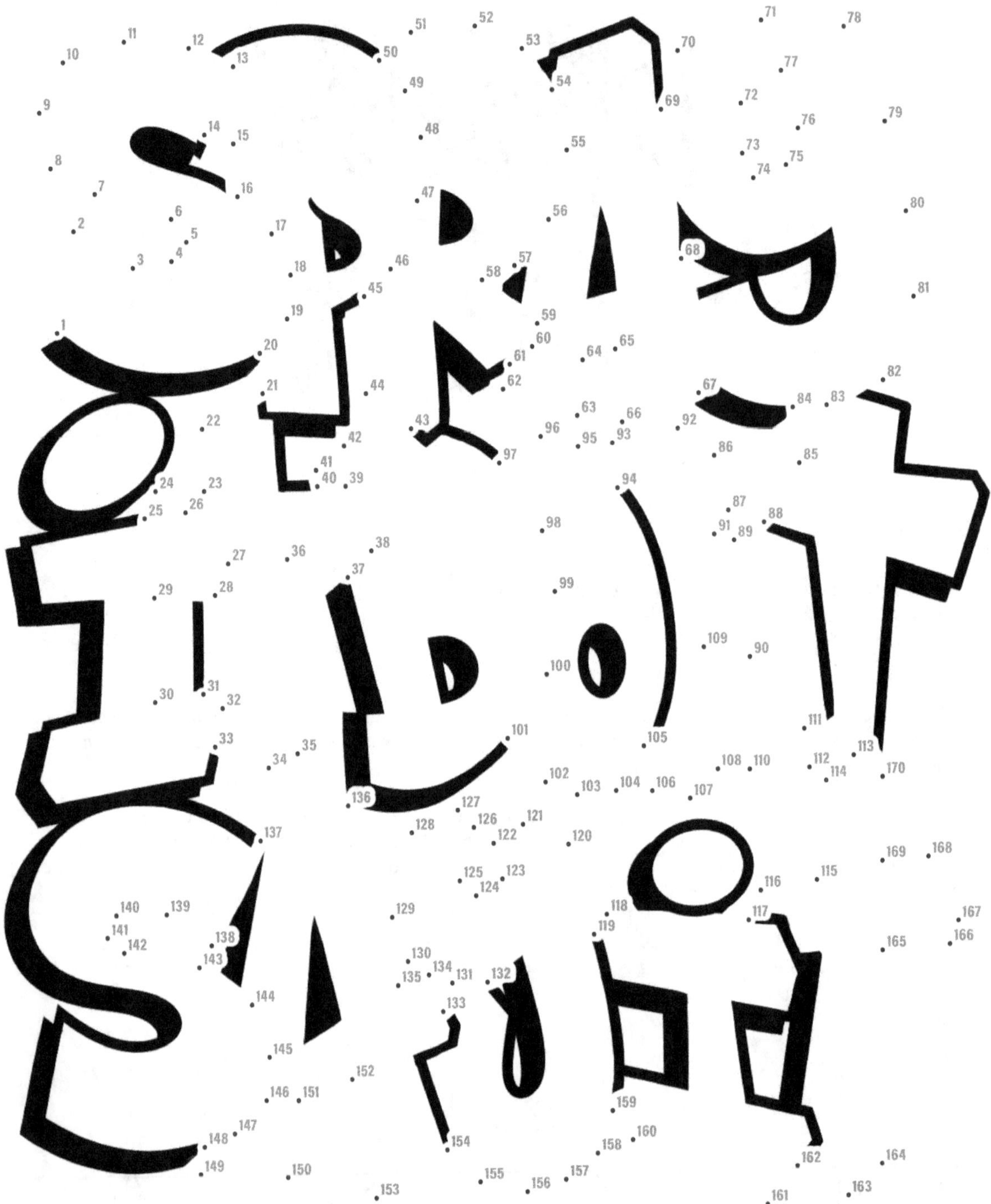

The History of Graffiti

SINCE HUMANS HAVE BEEN LIVING IN CAVES, THEY HAVE BEEN TELLING STORIES, WRITING ON THE WALLS.

Writing on the walls has been a constant in human history ever since we lived in caves and cooked around the fireplace. Since then, writing on the wall has been evolving, and today we mostly associate text on walls with the word; graffiti. Since the beginning of the hip-hop movement in the 70's, the graffiti community has grown worldwide. New words such as Toys, Crews, Tags, Pieces, Throw ups, Bombing, Outline and going All City. B boys and B girls popped up in every young person's vocabulary, and every telephone post and wall were scribbled upon - especially in the city where it all really started; New York. All train systems had graffiti on them, carrying the graffiti writer's artwork all the way from Manhattan to Brooklyn.

Graffiti was all about getting up, having your art seen, being more, being cool, being the best. Graffiti were all about being the best writer, doing the largest and most colorful pieces, executing the cleanest throw up in the least amount of time, having respect and giving respect. And the beauty of it is that still is all about that, that is what the graffiti community is all about. Graffiti and the hip-hop movement grew from the economic crisis in New York and other American larger cities were facing in the start 70's. It became a voice of the people who had been let down by a system. It became a language only they could read, and they were proud of it.

One of the people who has been considered a key person, the one who started it all some might say, is Demitrius, or as he was known on the street; Taki183. His nickname was Taki and he lived on 183rd street on Manhattan, and by putting these two names together, Demitrius made what is known as one of the world's first true graffiti tags. Taki183 was working as a delivery boy making his way up and down Manhattan all day, making it easy for him to make his tag along his delivery route. He is known in the graffiti community as the first real graffiti writer.

In the beginning of the 80's the graffiti community exploded in a positive way. Legendary writers such as BLADE, SEEN, DONDI, LEE and PHASE 2 dominated the scene, making some of the best burners in the world, and thus laying the foundation for what we call graffiti today. Graffiti was everywhere in music videos and commercials being shown all over the world; movies, magazines, and professional exhibitions in Amsterdam. The movie Wild Style was shown on television in 1982 and later the movie Style Wars and the subway art book came to the surface of the world. These movies, magazines, commercials, and books made graffiti go international, and the styles were set free all around the world to be developed by the future generations. Today, the internet has brought us all together, making it possible to see what styles that are practiced in New Zealand, LA, Copenhagen and South Africa making it possible to be inspired be each other.

In our perspective, graffiti should be all about having fun. Graffiti is about making letters dance, putting characteristic into these dancing letters by giving them "personalities". You can always tell what kind of a person a graffiti writer is just by looking at his letter styles. Are they aggressive? Are they funky? Are they bubbly and light or heavy and dark? All these things make you know a lot of that writer without even having spoken a word with them.

Painting graffiti should be like when a jazz pianist improvises. The musician makes a note that leads him to another note, and another note until he has a chord. This chord can now be the basis for the song he is about to compose. Now he must add the right amount of extra style here and there, go back and forth some time, turn it around. Work on it. Work on it some more until it's finally done. Painting graffiti is kind of the same thing; you make a line that has a flow that will turn into a block. You make another block, turn and twist that around and now you have the letter P. This P needs some friends, so you must make some for it until you have a word. You try some different letters - putting them in, taking them out, flipping it around and at some point, you will have it, it just feels right, you have your first tag.

When you start making graffiti, we encourage you to talk with your friends about graffiti, send each other flicks and inspire each other to become better. Make a graffiti crew, go out and paint together. Learn all the rules from the masters, study their pieces, throw ups and hand styles - and then forget everything you have learned about graffiti - go out and make what YOU think graffiti is! What impact will your graffiti art have on the graffiti community in your hometown? Your region? Country? The whole graffiti world? Welcome to the graffiti community.

Vocabulary

3D STYLE
Graffiti piece that has a three dimensional illusion.

ABSTRACT STYLE
A style of painting where it's not about painting letters, but rather showcasing your technical and color skills.

ALL-CITY
A label you can gain by becoming a famous writer in your entire city. "That guy went all-city!".

ANGEL(S)
Respected and famous writers who have passed away.

ANTI-STYLE
Also know as ugly style, or ignorant style. A style of painting where you deliberately paint toy-ish making it "ugly" to look at.

BACKJUMP
A quickly executed graffiti piece. Often made on a breifly parked train.

BACK TO BACK
Graffiti that covers the entirety of the wall or train from end to end.

BEEF
Conflict between writers. "Yea, they have a beef going on".

BLACK BOOK
A sketchbook for your sketches and pieces. Also known as a "piece book".

BLOCKBUSTERS
Easy readable throw up letters.

BITE
To steal another writers work, name, color schemes or style.

BOMBING
When you hit an area hard with graffiti. "We bombed that neighbourhood".

BUBBLE STYLE
A graffiti style using rounded letters where it looks as if the letters have been blown up as balloons.

BURNER
A really good graffiti piece. "Yea, it's a real burner!".

BUFFING
Removing graffiti from a surface with a pressure washer e.g.

CALLIGRAFFITI
Graffiti that draws inspiration from calligraphy.

CAP
Nozzle/tip part of an aerosol spray can - where the paint comes out.

CAPPING
Destroying other writers work by painting lines on it. "The pieces got capped this weekend".

CARTOON/CHARACTER
A figure or famous cartoon painted next to your piece.

CLEAN LINES
Smooth lines without edges, dust or drips.

CREW
A group of graffiti writers working under the same crewname.

DEF
Something really good.

DRIPS
Paint flowing from your lines as you paint. Can be intentional or unintentional.

DUSTY LINES
Unclean lines that comes from spraying too far away from the wall.

FADING
A color blending technique.

FILL-IN
The color combination inside the letters.

FREESTYLE
Freestyle writing is painting a piece without having a sketch prepared from home.

GHOST
A graffiti piece that has been buffed but is still a bit visible on the wall.

GOING OVER
Painting over another writers graffiti piece.

GETTING UP
Painting.

HALL OF FAME
A location with many walls that graffiti writers visit to paint pieces, throw ups and tags.

HANDSTYLE
Your font when writing your tag.

HEAVEN SPOT
A place that is difficult or dangerous to paint thus also difficult to buff. Gives credit from other writers if you paint these spots.

KING/QUEEN
A graffiti writer who is highly respected amongst other graffiti writers.

MARRIED COUPLE
Two fully painted train cars that are located side by side.

MOP
A homemade marker. Usually made from an old deodorant and filt.

OLD SCHOOL
A term that refers to the 70's and 80's where the hip hop culture began.

ONE
A graffiti writers tag.

PIECE
A graffiti writers tag made with complex letters including a lot of details. Comes from the word masterpiece.

RACK
To steal.

ROLLER GRAFFITI
Graffiti pieces that are painted on large surfaces using rollers and bucket paint.

ROOFTOP
A piece painted from the top of a roof, onto the mural of the neighbour building.

RUN
How much time a graffiti piece survives on a surface. "That piece ran for only two months".

SEMI WILDSTYLE
A less complex style of wildstyle.

SOAKER TAGS
Tags made with ink filled fire extinguishers. Often made in huge scale with lots of drips.

STREET ART
Art made on the street often with stencils and containing a message towards the society.

TAG
A graffiti writers alias.

THROW UP
A graffiti writers tag made with easy readable letters, often bubble letters or blockbuster letters.

TOY
An inexperienced writer with poor or bad style. Come from the saying "trouble on your system".

URBAN ART
Summarizes all visual art forms in urban space – both streeet art and graffiti.

YARD
Where the trains are parked at night.

WHOLECAR
A fully painted train cart.

WILDSTYLE
Complex graffitiletters that are difficult, close to impossible to read.

WHOLETRAIN
All train cars fully painted from first to last car in the train composition.

WRITER
A person who paints graffiti. "Does he write? Yes, he is a writer".

WINDOW DOWN
A train car painted with graffiti from the windows and down.

Equipment & SURFACES

When talking graffiti and equipment it doesn't take much to get started, you could grab a pencil right now and start doing graffiti! With that being said, there are some essentials I think you should invest in.

A SET OF PAINTINGCLOTHES
You can use when you paint. No matter how hard you try not to get paint on your clothes, paint always finds a way anyhow.

A STACKABLE PLASTIC BOX
To transport your paint and can be used to gain some extra height.

A BLACKBOOK
To collect your sketches and pieces.

SPRAY PAINT
Of high quality which means you shouldn't buy the stuff from a carpenter store. You can get high pressure, low pressure, mat and glossy paint and it's difficult to say what you will prefer. Go to your local graffiti store and buy some different kinds the first time and try for yourself!

DIFFERENT CAPS
For different kinds of work.

MARKERS AND PENCILS
Of different kinds.

A CAMERA
To take pictures of everything you make. In some years from now, you will appreciate having documented your process.

A MASK
Is absolutely necessary when painting graffiti as the vapours contain solvents that can be hazardous to your health. Buy a decent gasmask with active filters, instead of the disposable ones.

A TABLET
Is a great tool for sketching, when you are on the go. Using a tablet for sketching and drawing also gives you more possibilities for skewing, distorting and playing around with your letters.

GLOVES
To prevent paint on your hands, and the solvents from the paint entering through your bloodstreams. Could either be thin latex gloves or padded rubber gloves.

A WALL
To practice on, either one, you build yourself or a legal one in your community.

INSPIRATION
To keep you motivated! Follow your graffiti heroes on Instagram and buy graffiti magazines and books!

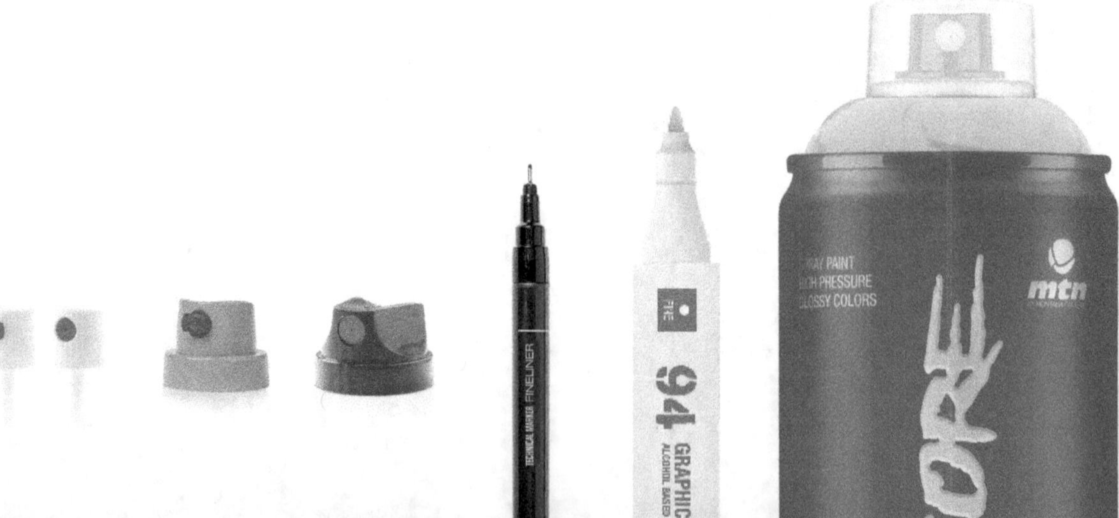

Graffiti can be painted anywhere, but how the paint reacts, how it looks, how much it absorbs and how long it will last on the wall depends on the surface - and of course the weather conditions.

CONCRETE

Is great to paint on, especially if it has a painted undercoat. Concrete surfaces absorb a small amount of the paint making clean fill-ins possible and easy to avoid drips, if you focus.

GLASS

Doesn't absorb paint at all making it difficult to avoid drips and makes your lines look like they are painted in uneven layers. If you look at the glass from behind after you have painted, you will see your piece backwards, and the first lines you did being most visible - you can make cool effects with this.

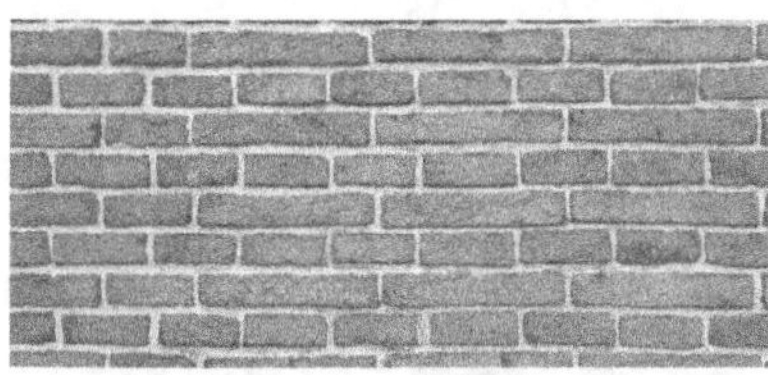

BRICK

Is similar to concrete - works best if you make an undercoat of primer before painting, but will also work fine without. You can even take the raw brick background and incorporate in your piece.

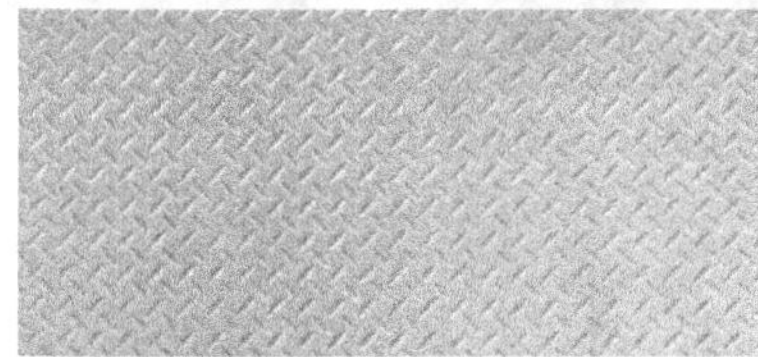

METAL

Resembles glass as it doesn't absorb paint at all. If you master to apply the paint in even layers you will find yourself using less paint on surfaces likes this.

WOOD

If untreated, old or rotten will absorb paint more, than if the wood has been treated or gotten an undercoat.

How To: TAGS

GETTING STARTED

A tag is a personal street name of a graffiti writer, also called a "one". The true identity behind a writer's tag is usually known only by good friends and crew members so don't tell it to everyone you meet. Your tag follows you throughout your whole graffiti career, therefore it takes a lot of consideration when choosing the one you will go for. Change your tag once a week, go through all the letters in the alphabet and work especially on the letters you like the least. Sometimes you will get surprised how each letter evolves when you give them some time.

FACTS

→ KEEP IT SHORT!
Tags are usually between 4-6 letters.

→ KEEP IT PERSONAL!
Your tag represents your unique style and sets you apart from other writers.

→ KEEP YOUR TAG!
Once you've chosen your final tag, don't change it or you'll lose the fame you've built with it

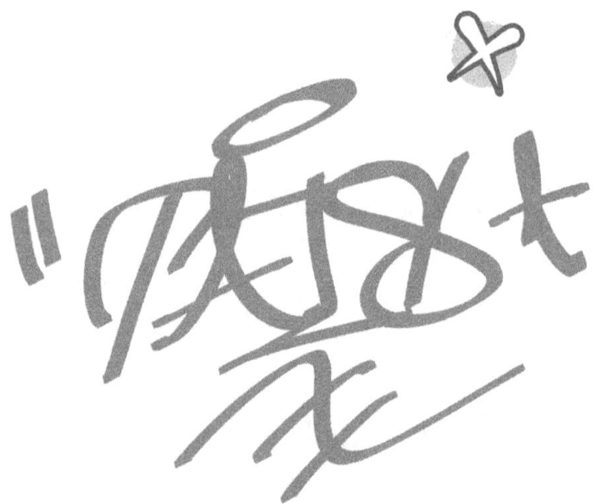

This tag has to many forced style elements on it, making the overall appearance stressed and messy. A writer who made a tag like this would be called 'a toy'.

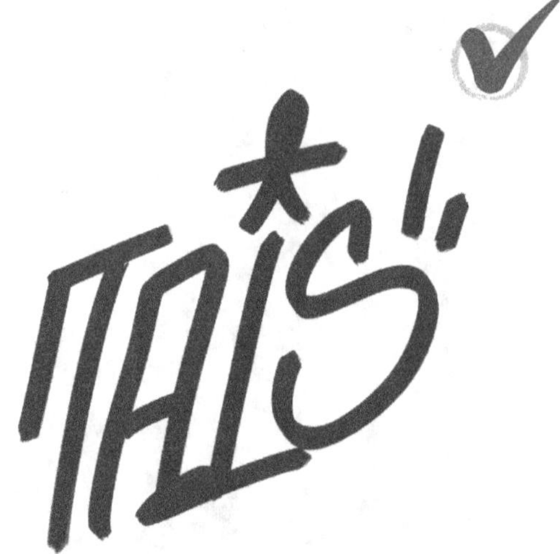

This tag follows an overall direction, has few controlled style elements added that compliments the relatively simple letters. A great example of a well-executed tag.

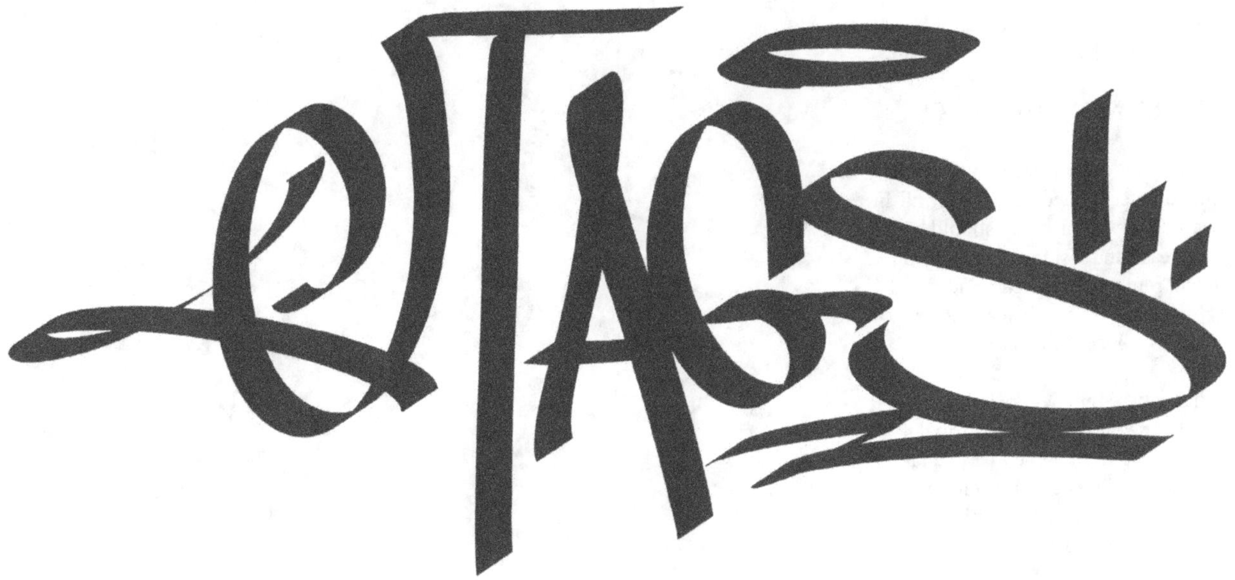

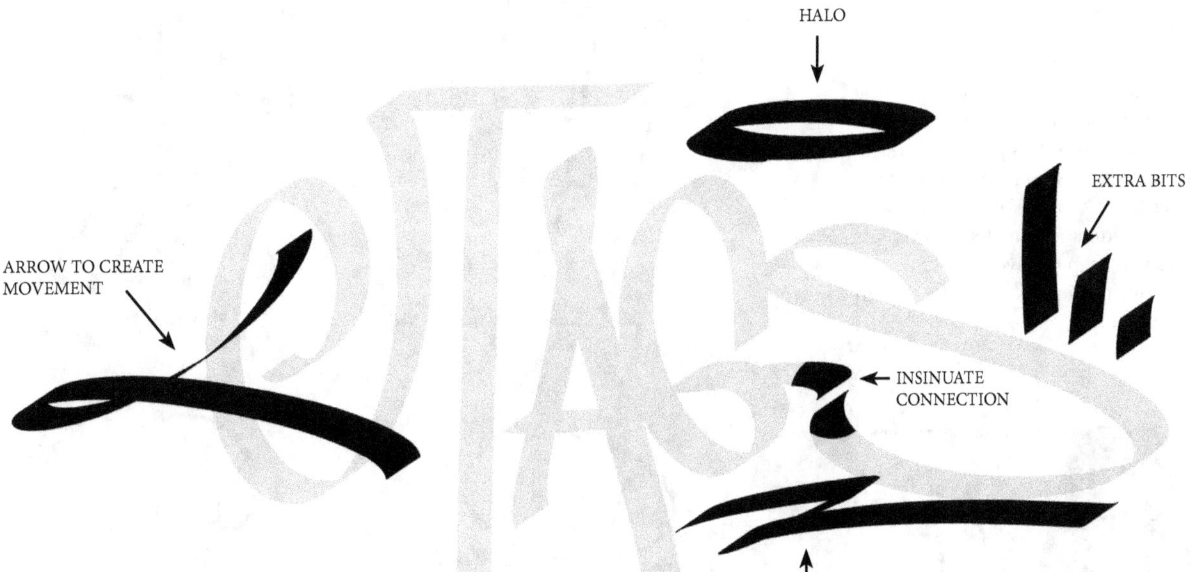

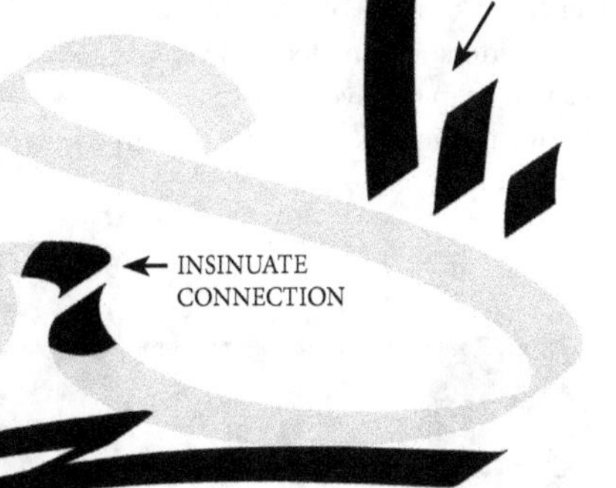

HALO
EXTRA BITS
ARROW TO CREATE
MOVEMENT
INSINUATE
CONNECTION
ZIGZAC LINE

How To: 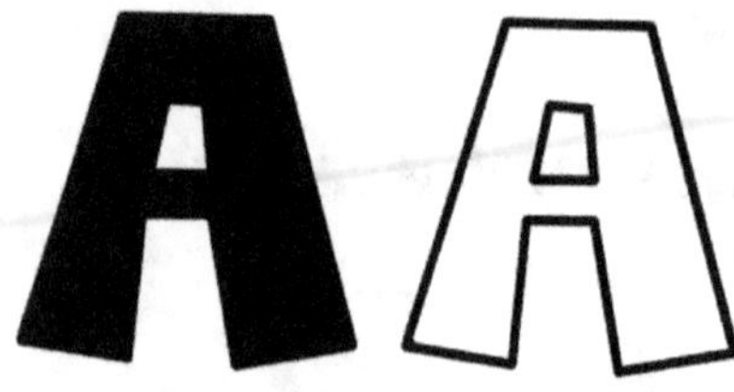 THROW-UPS

UNDERSTAND THE BASICS

A throw up is a writer's tag made with outlined letters added single color fill-in and a shadow. A throw-up should be simple, easy and fast to do, something you will remember by heart and could just 'throw up' on a wall at any given moment – hence the name.

To make these bubble-like letters, you take the outline from a normal handstyle letter. Imagine that you take the handstyle letter and blow it up like a balloon. Now we can play with fill-ins, shadows, drips and cracks.

THE LOG RULE

To make these letters in the beginning, you can use the log-rule. The log-rule is dividing the letters parts and areas into shapes/logs, so the whole letter is easier to make sense of – like if you were making letters with matches. This rule helps you keep the overview of where and how many parts of a letter that are overlappinig.

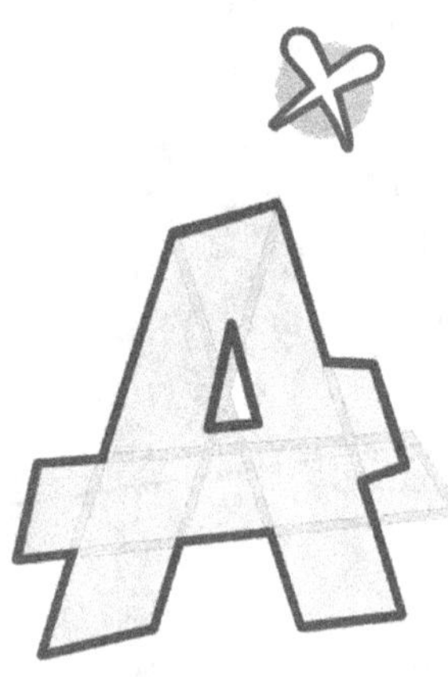

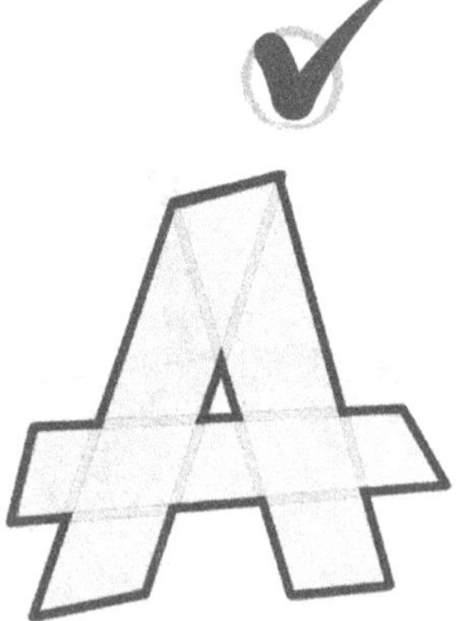

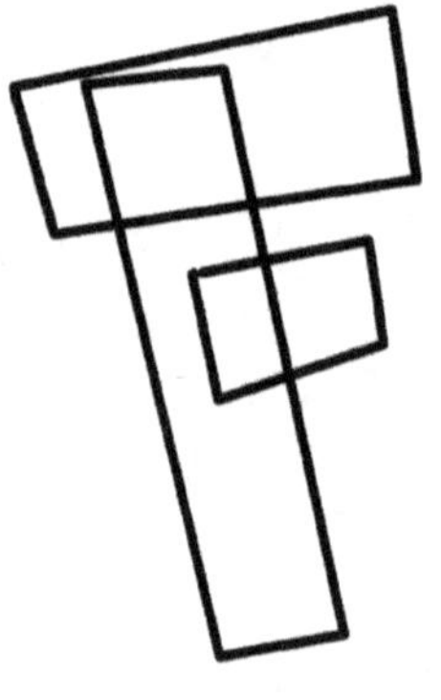

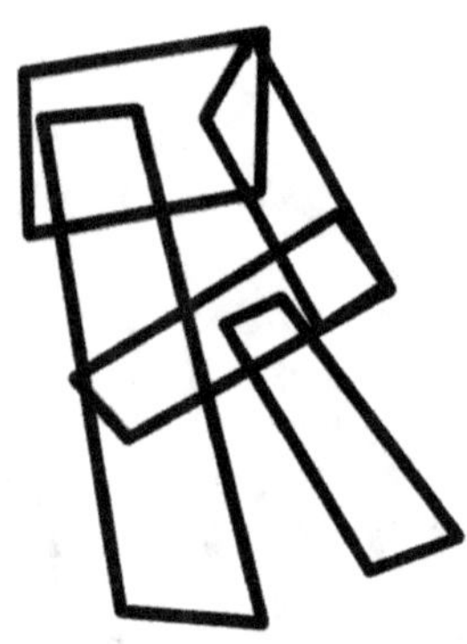

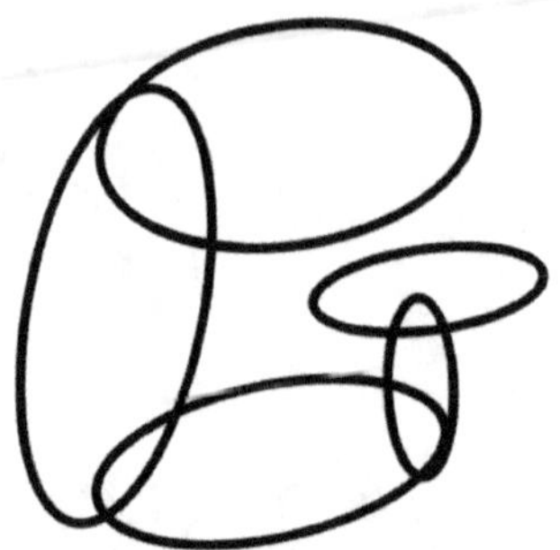

↑ Outline from regular handstyle-letter

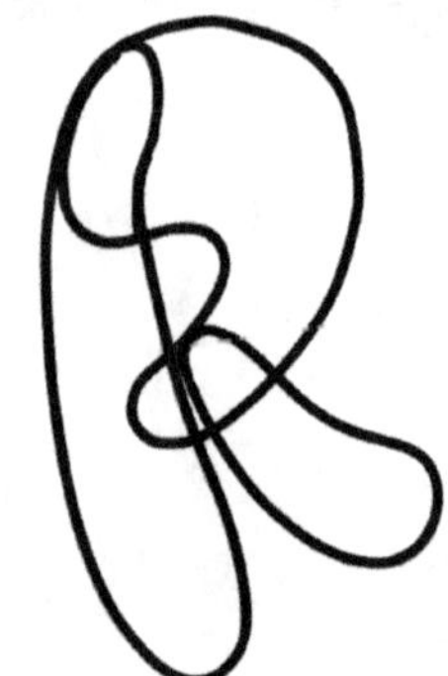

FILL-IN

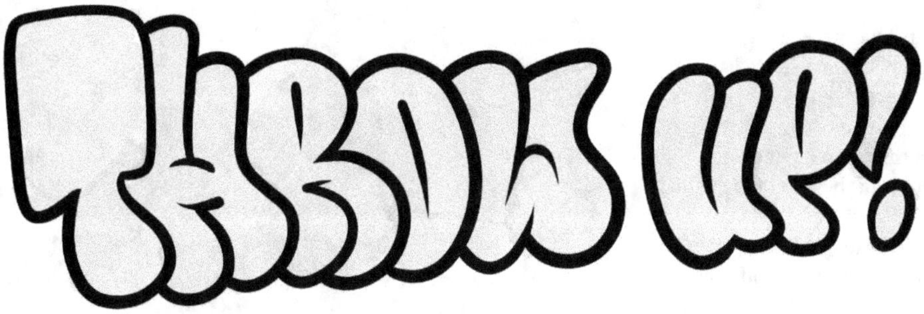

OUTLINE

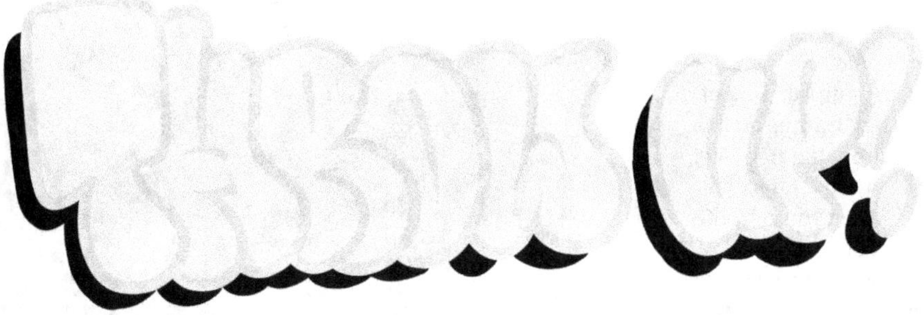

SHADOW

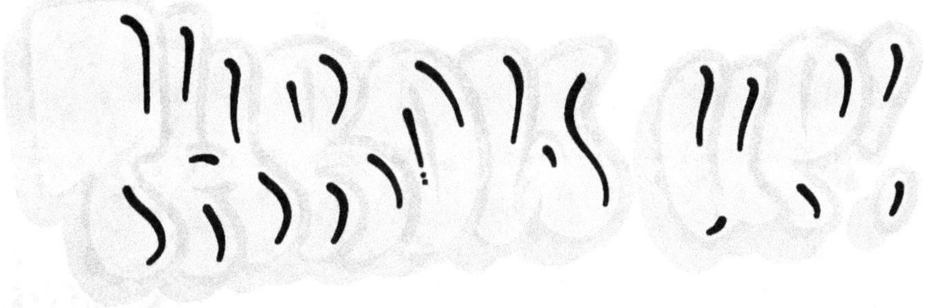

HIGHLIGHT

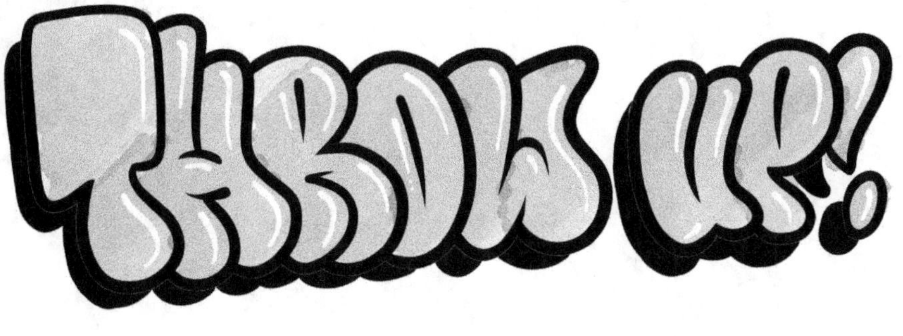

THROW-UP

How To: Pieces

UNDERSTANDING A PIECE

A piece, short for masterpiece, is a graffiti writer's ONE made with complicated and colorful letters. A piece is where the writer's style shines through. It's more time consuming than a throw up due to the higher level of details in the letters such as arrows, cracks, blocks, cuts and wild color combinations. A well-executed piece gives more respect from other writers and is considered something experienced writers do.

Before you start making your own pieces, grab a graffiti magazine and copy as many pieces as you can. By copying the work of others, you get to practice drawing graffiti pieces and letter structure without having the pressure of having to make something from scratch yourself. When you copy the work of others, be sure not to take credit for it. It should be for the mere purpose of practice. If you claim that it's your own work, it would be called biting.

TIPS

Build graffiti pieces letters with the log rule in mind, just like when making throw up letters!

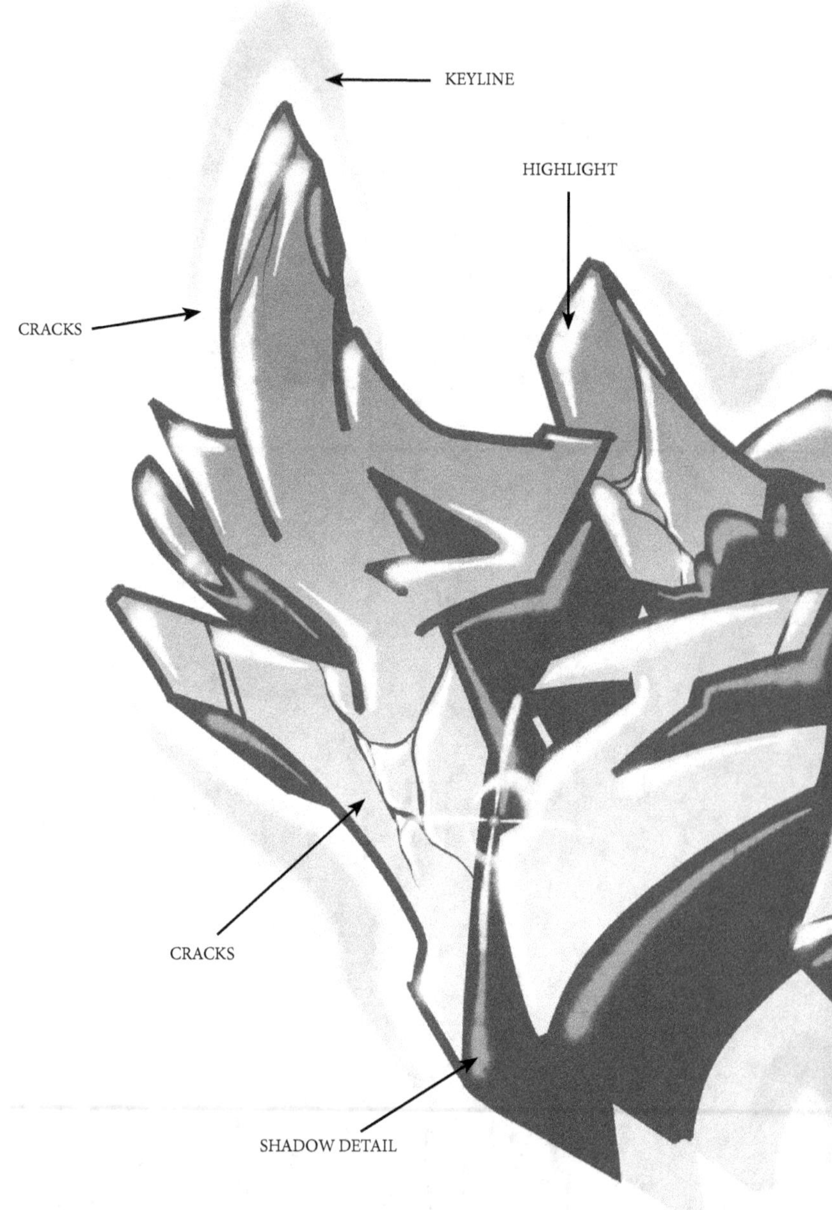

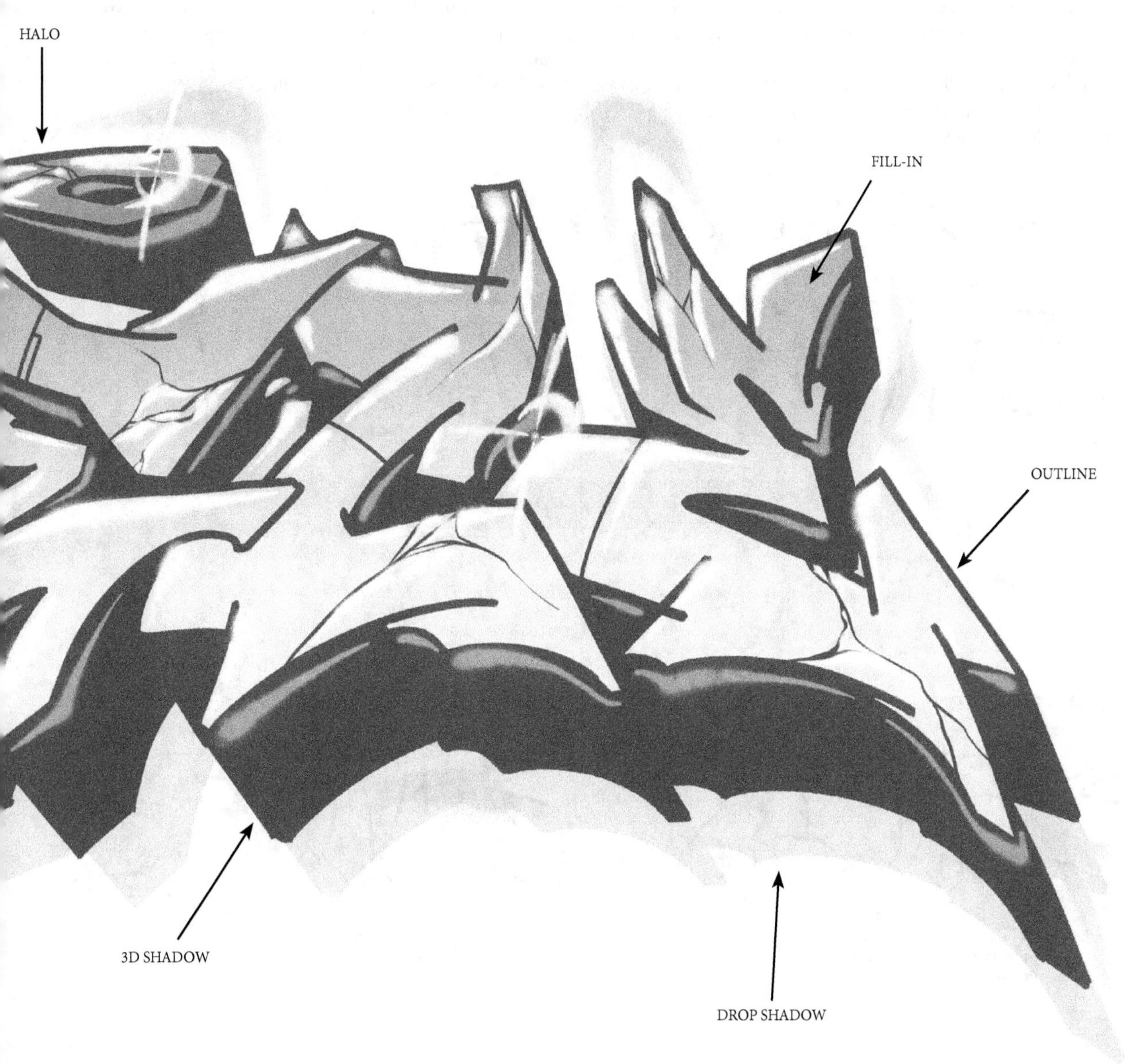

HALO
FILL-IN
OUTLINE
3D SHADOW
DROP SHADOW

Make Your Own 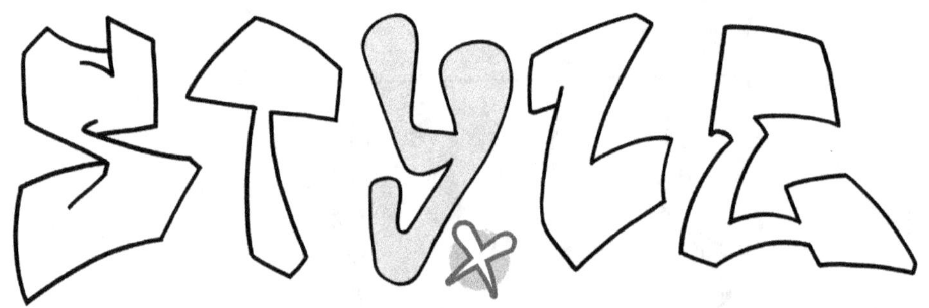

When starting to make your own pieces from scratch, create each letter separately before combining them. Add the same style to each letter so the overall style of the upcoming piece is coherent. You want to avoid making one letter only with round shapes and then the next only with hard edges. The higher pursuit is to combine different styles, so they compliment each other, but be careful not to overdo it at the beginning – less is more.

When each one of your letters are made, combine them into one piece. Turn, twist and make them overlap each other, so they become one whole in the best possible way. After you have combined them, you can add extra details to fill in the negative space such as drips, blocks, cracks and shadows. We will look more into this in chapter 6 and 7.

The round-shaped **Y** doesn't go with hard-edged letters – always try to follow the same style throughout your sketch!

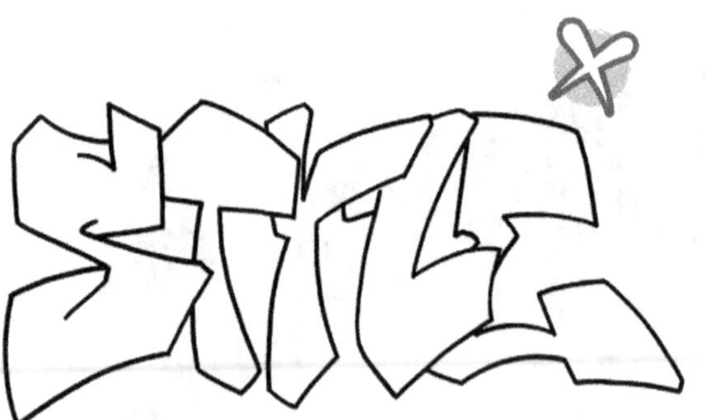

When you've created all your letters, combine them into one piece. Turn, twist and make them overlap each other until they fit together in the best possible way.

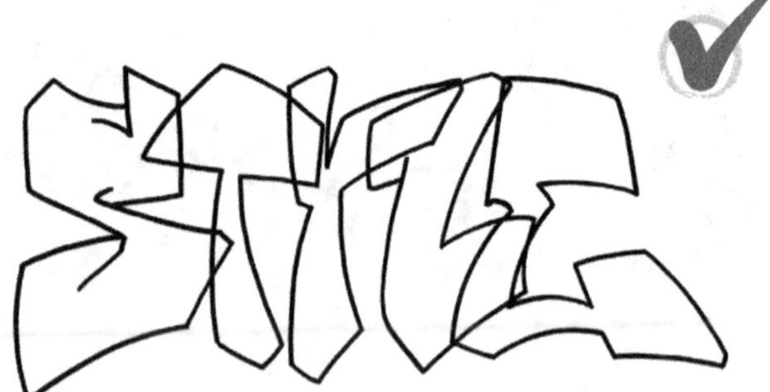

Letters combined without connecting the piece hides key areas

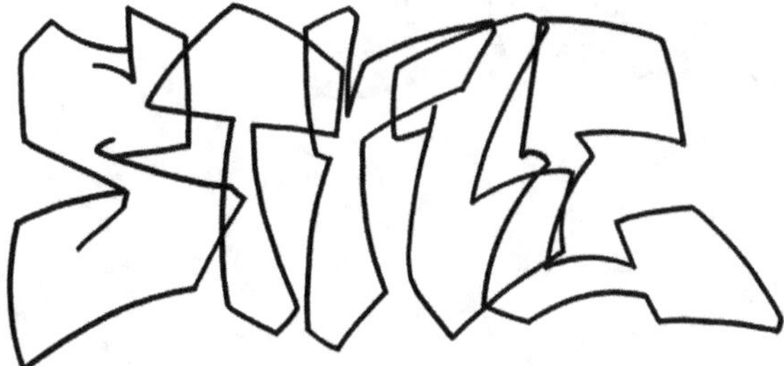

Combined letters connect the piece.

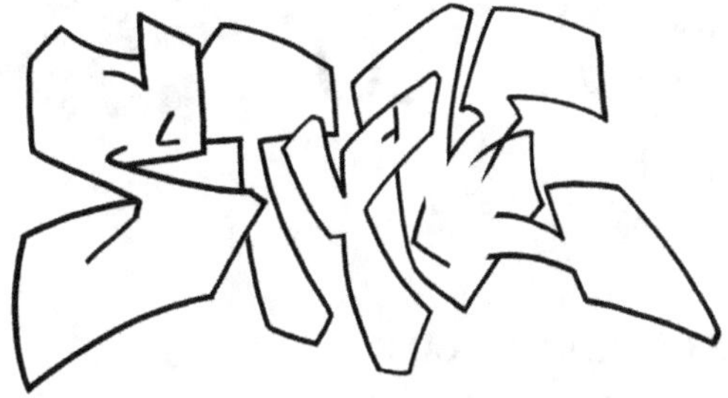

Erase some of the overlapping lines without erasing the key areas of each letter.

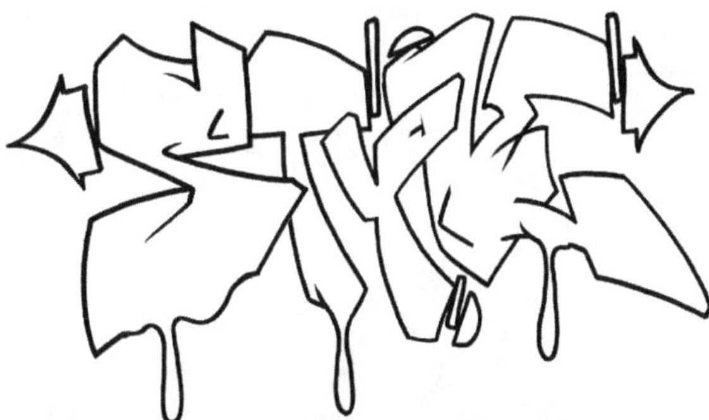

When the letters have been combined, add extra details such as drips, blocks and shadows to fill in the negative space.

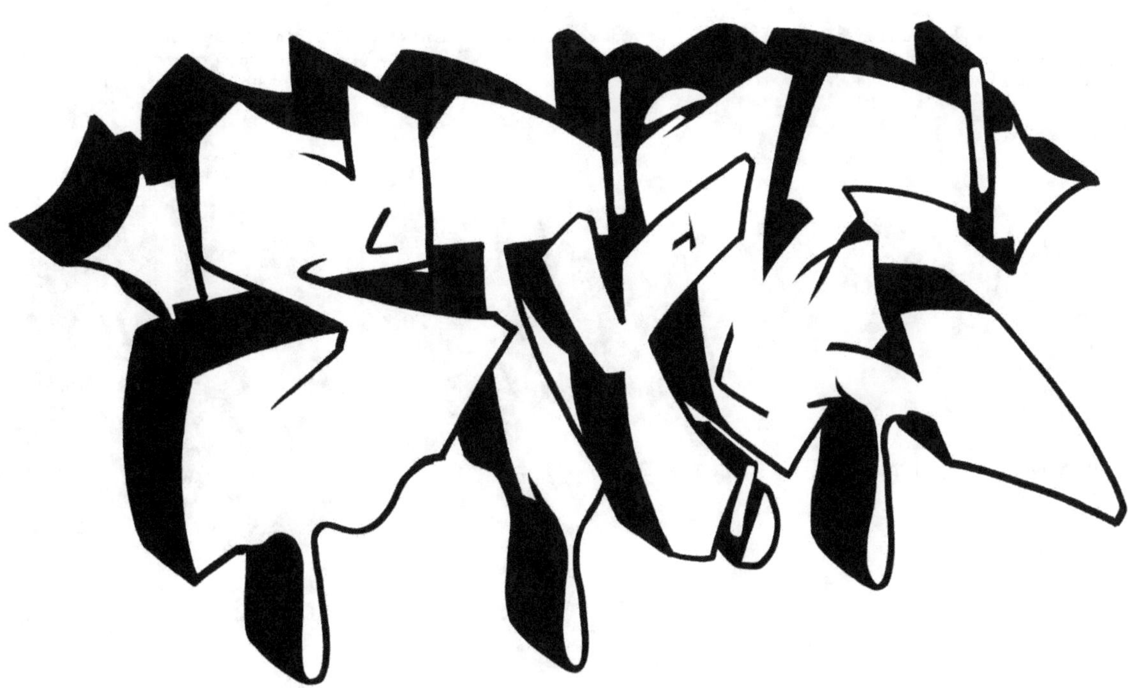

How to: 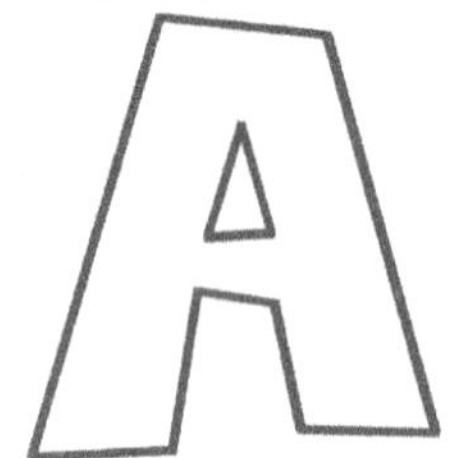

ESSENTIAL IN GRAFFITI

Shadows are essential to the overall expression of your Piece or Throw Up.
They add depth and makes your work a lot more interesting to look at.
There are two overall approaches for making different shadows.
Drop down- and 3D-shadows.

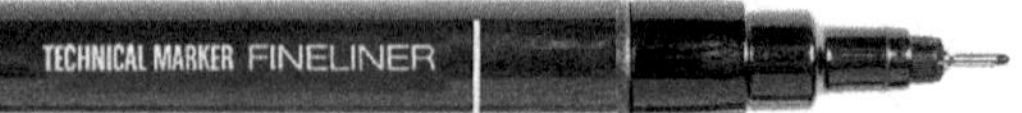

1. Outline of a plain letter.

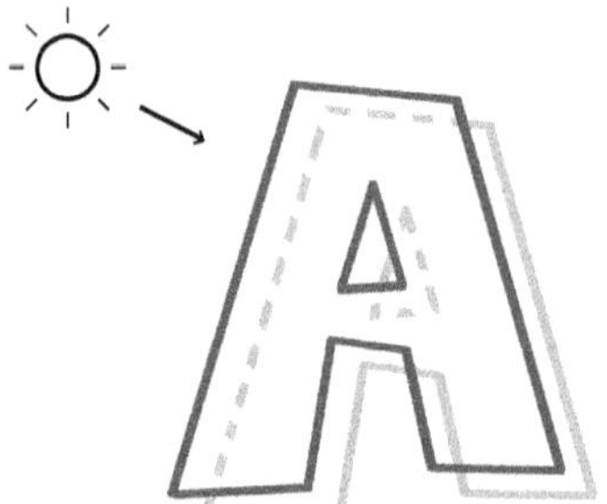

2. Duplicate the letter and place it at an angle.
It helps to imagine the letter being lit by the
sun – the dropshadow is what you want to
draw!

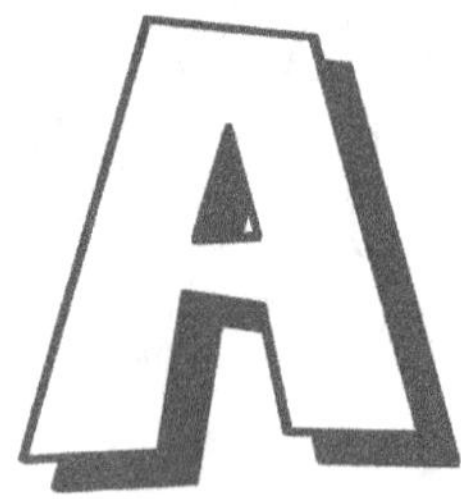

3. Fill the shadow and the dropdown is now
complete.

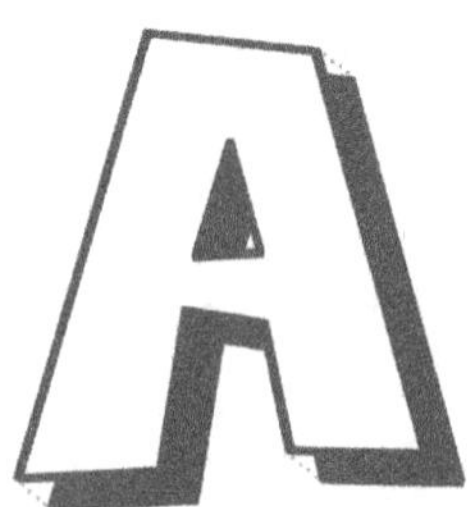

4. For a 3-dimensional look, connect the corners of
the letters to the corners of the shadow as illustrated
by the dotted lines. Make sure the lines are parallel
for a realistic feeling.

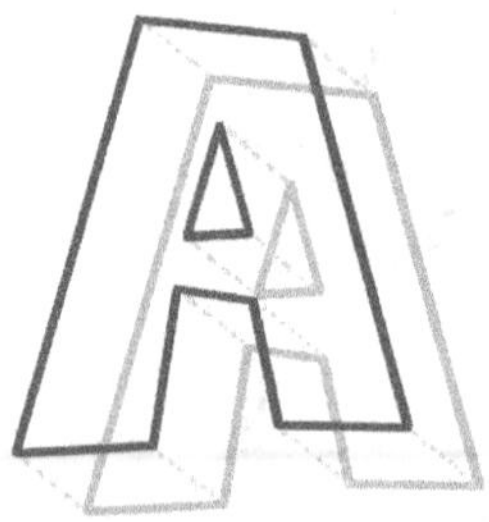

5. The letter before fill-in. The dots illustrate the
position of the shadow.

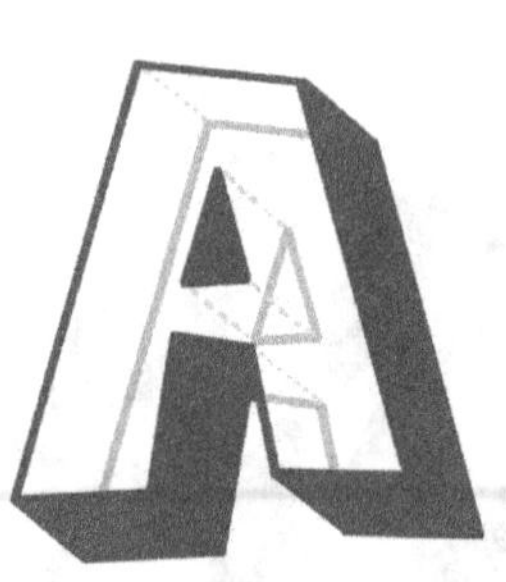

6. Filled-in shadow.

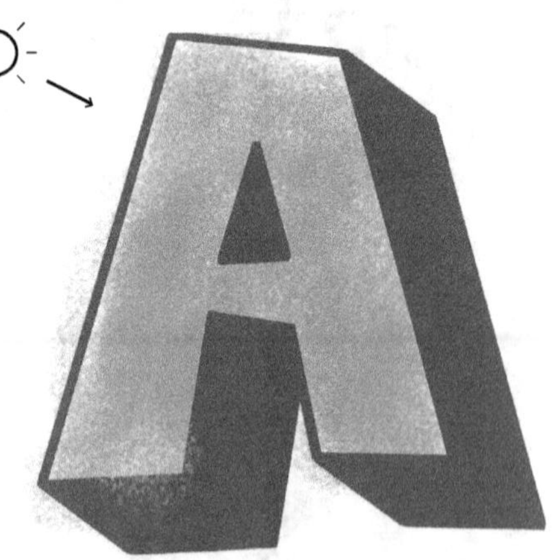

7. The finished 3D-shadow without guiding dots.

COMMON SHADOW MISTAKES

Here you can see some common mistakes students make the
first time trying to make a 3D shadow.

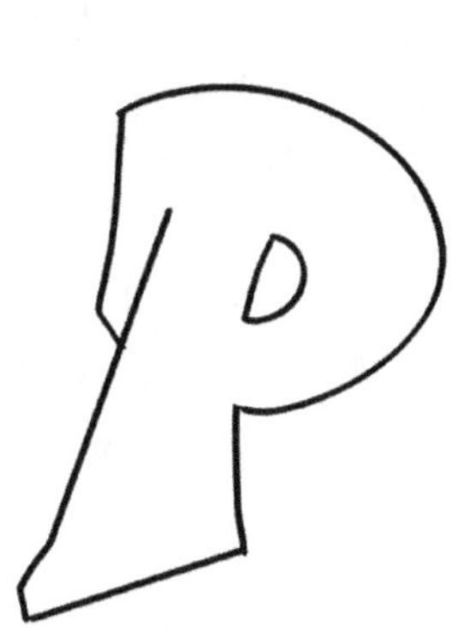

Outline of letter

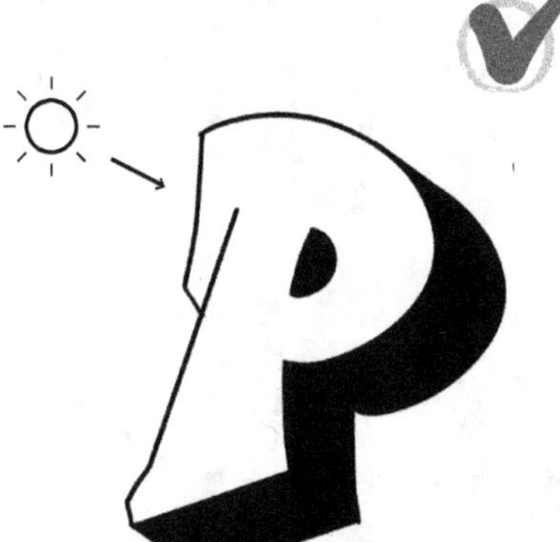

3D shadow made correctly.

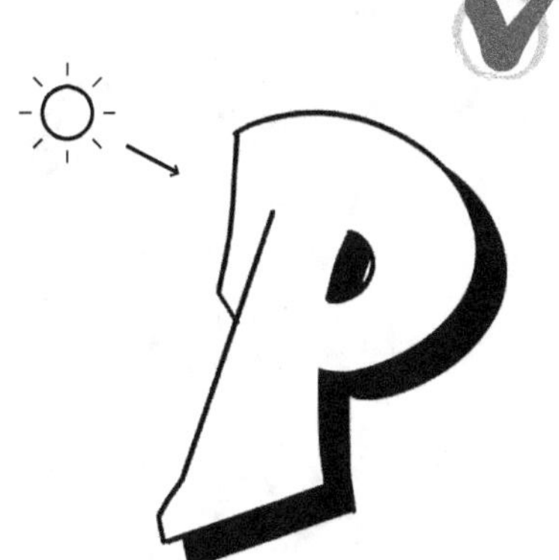

Dropdown shadow made correctly

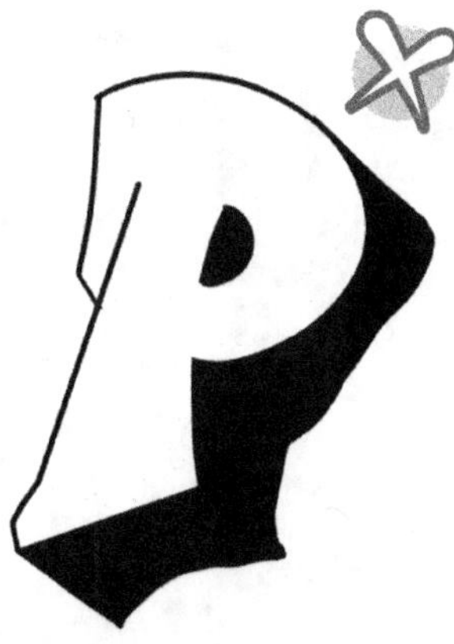

3D shadow-lines not following the
original outline.

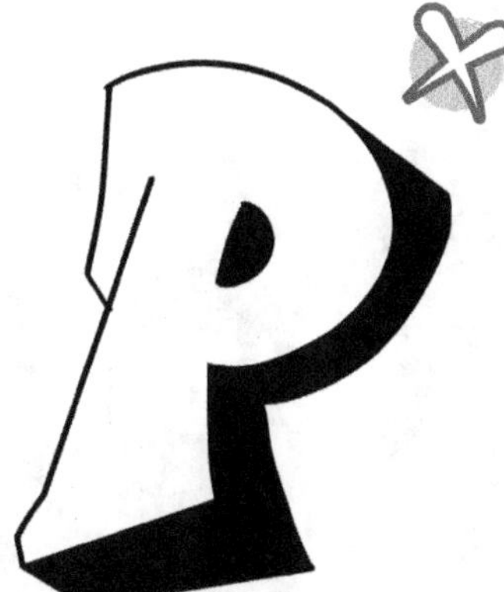

3D shadow-lines with different lengths
resulting in a wrong connection of the
original outline.

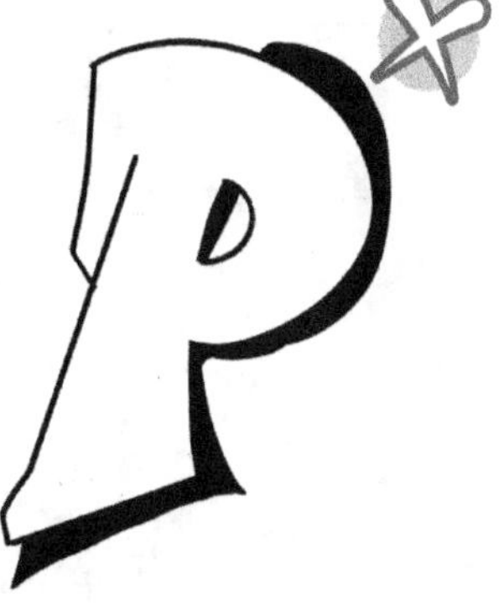

Dropdown shadow-lines no following
the rule of duplicating the original
outline.

TIPS

Light a flashlight on your hand. The shadow your hand
casts is a drop-down shadow! Experiment with moving
the flashlight around to create different shadow angles.

WHEEL OF SHADOW

Here you can see the same letter being lit from 8
different directions and how each shadow would look
like accordingly. Inner circle is 3D-shadows and outer
circle is drop-down shadows. Return to this wheel for
future shadow reference.

EXERCISE

Make a wheel of shadows
on the letter S.

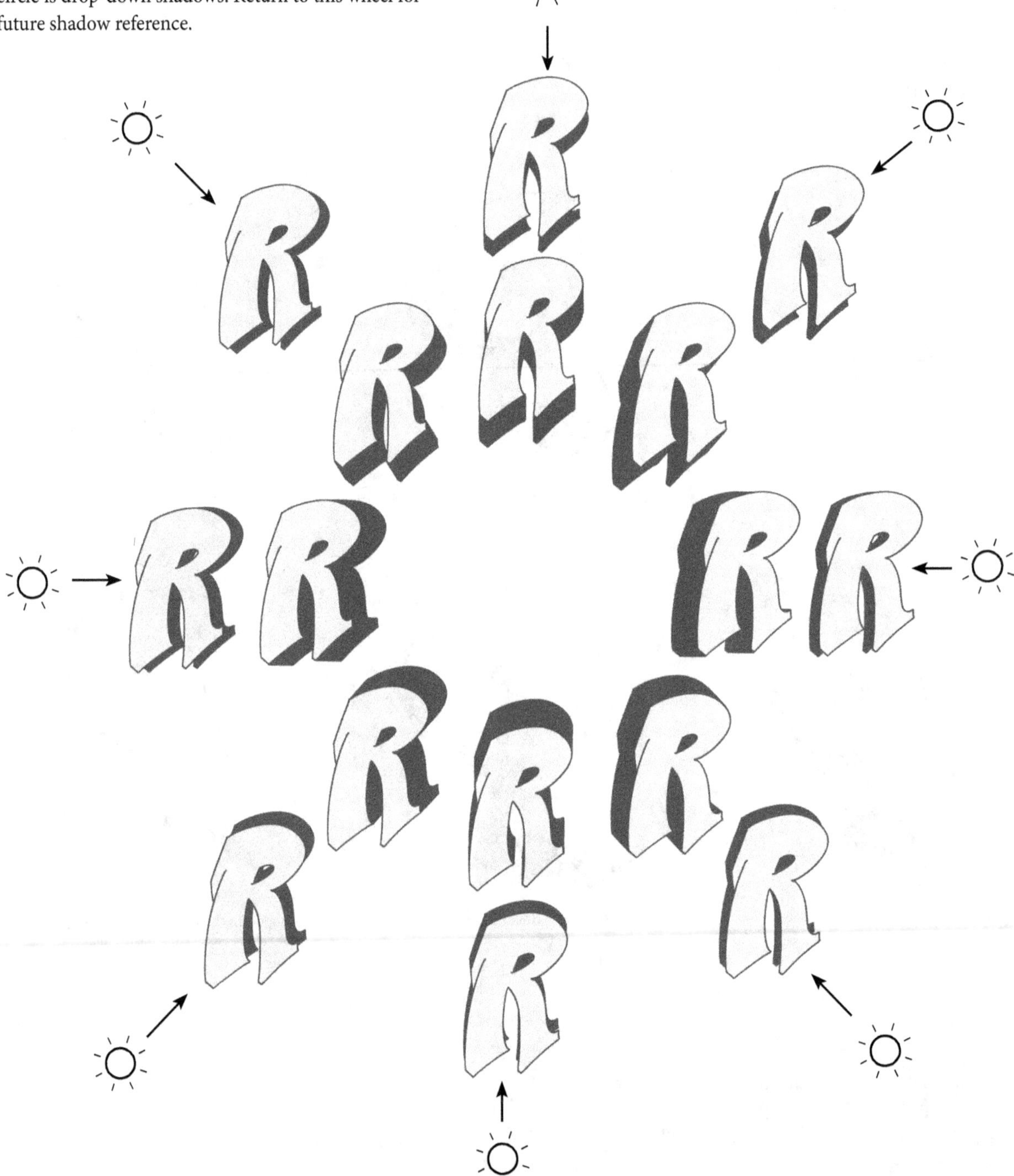

ADD SHADOW TO A PIECE

When adding shadow to a piece and not just one letter, view the piece as one coherent shape and draw the shadows accordingly. This means that the letters of each shadow shouldn't be in front of the next letter coming.

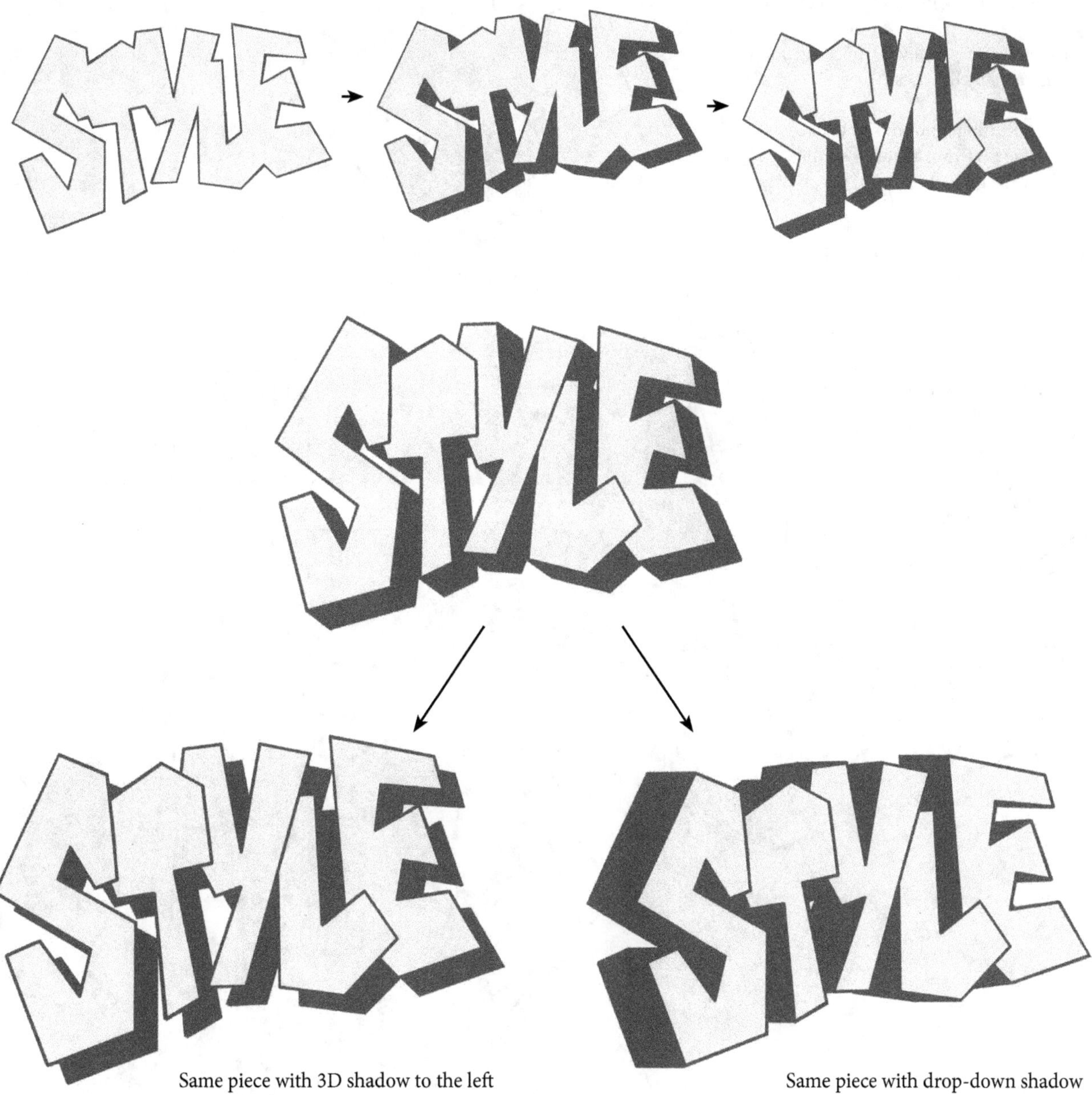

Same piece with 3D shadow to the left

Same piece with drop-down shadow

Vanishing Point

VANISHING POINT SHADOW

These shadows follow a vanishing point illustrated by the dots.

The vanishing point can be located anywhere on your sketch – simply follow the guidelines for 3D-shadows.

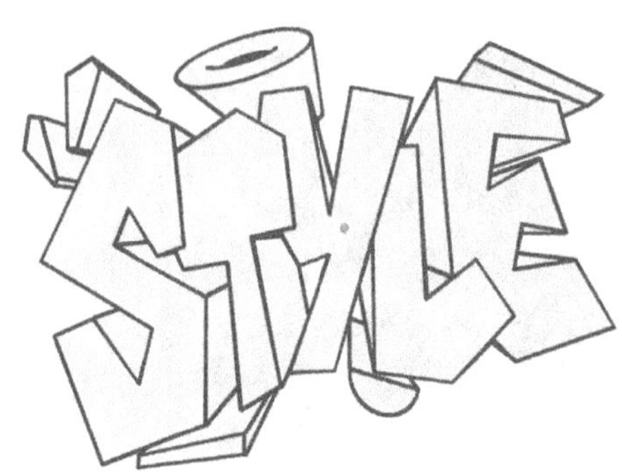

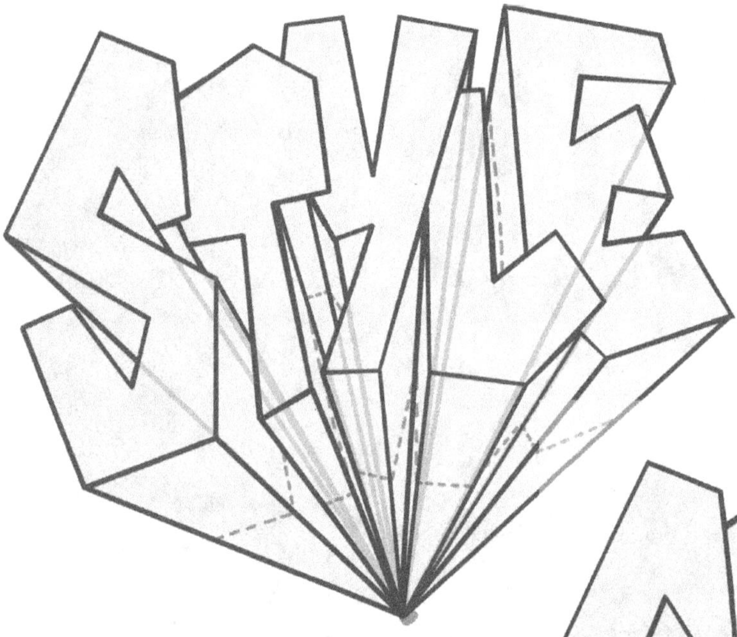

EXERCISE

Make the different shadows from this and the previous page on your own piece

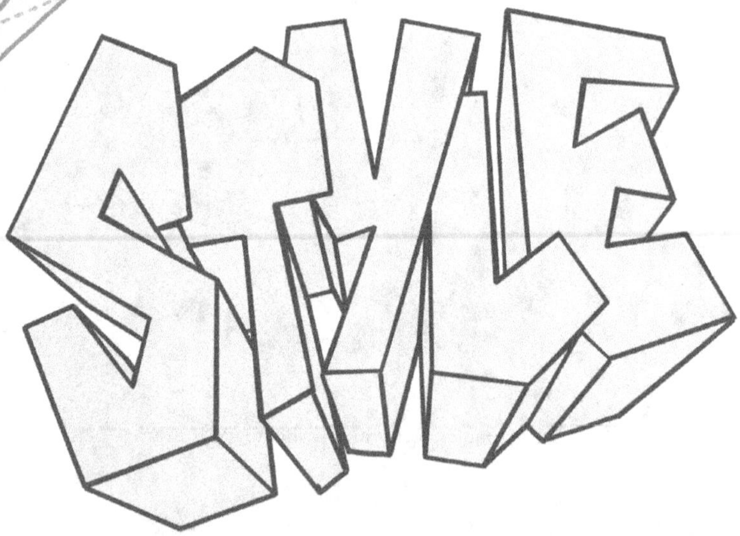

Key Areas

REMEMBER THE ESSENTAILS

When making throw ups, pieces or even tags, it's important, that your letters don't overlap each other, so they hide the most important parts of the letter behind. These parts are the lines in the letters that make them identifiable. These are called key areas. To the right you see an alphabet drawn with block letters, where the black lines are the key areas of the letter. This alphabet should be seen as a guideline to key areas and isn't a final answer. You can overlap some of the red lines in each letter and still be able to identify them, but it depends on the sketch. Try for yourself to see what works.

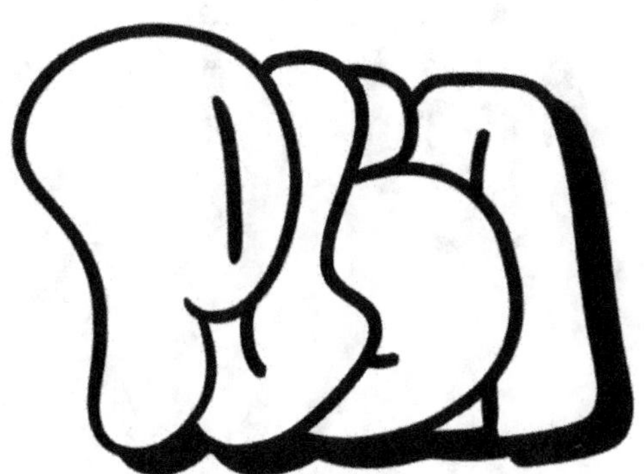

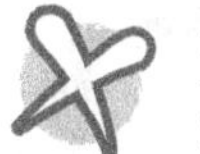

Key areas have NOT been in consideration when making this throw up. Letters after P is difficult to identify

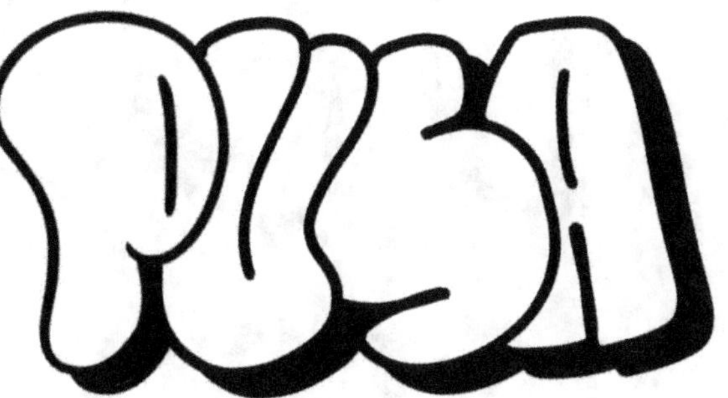

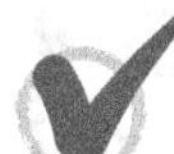

Key areas have been in consideration when making this throw up. Letters are easily recognizable.

ABCDE
FGHIJ
KLMNO
PQRST
UVWXYZ

A B C D E

F G H I J

K L M N O

P Q R S T

U V W X Y Z

A B C
G H I J
N O P
T U V W

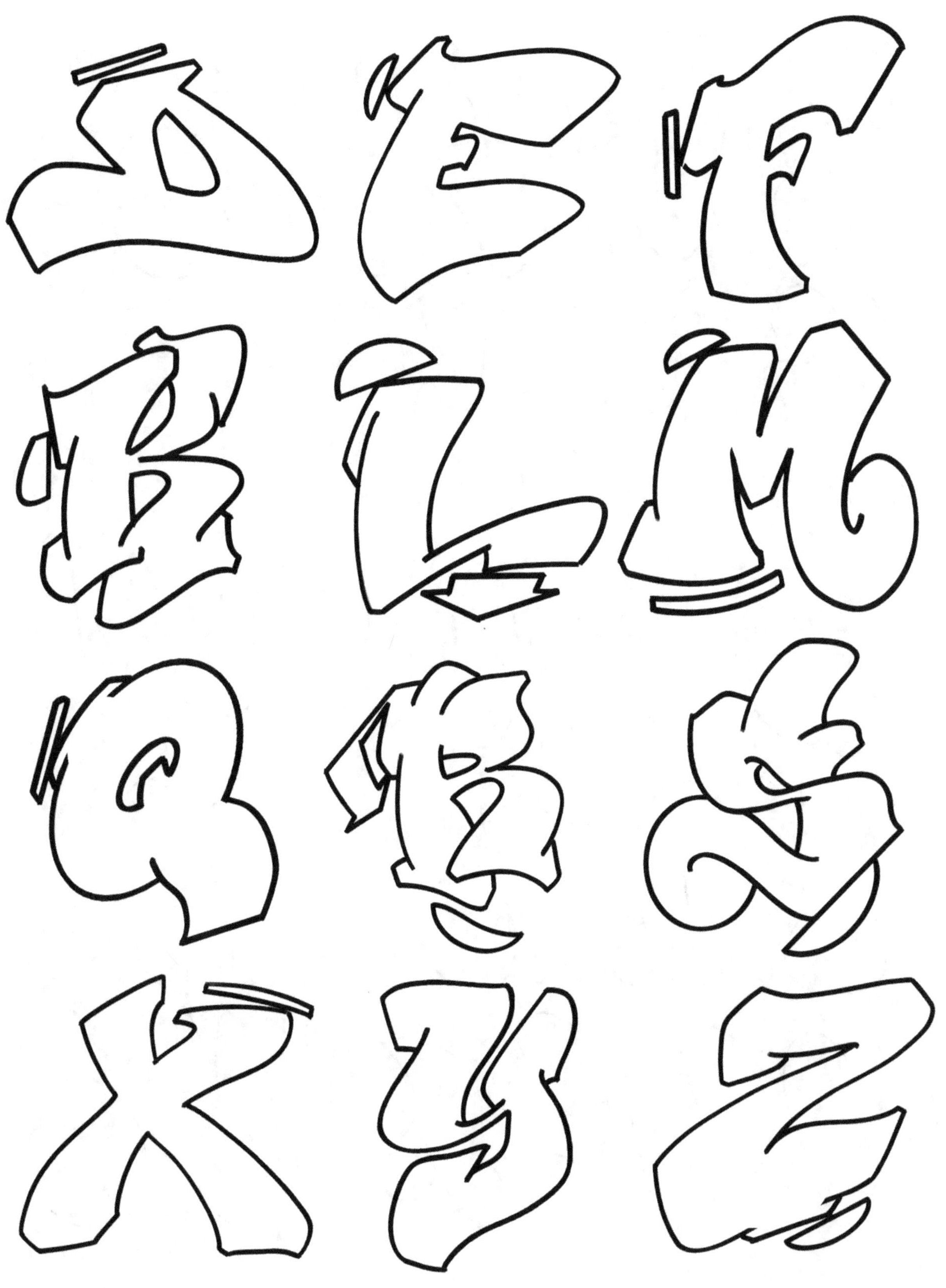

A B C D E

F G H I J

K L M N O

P Q R S T

U V W X Y Z

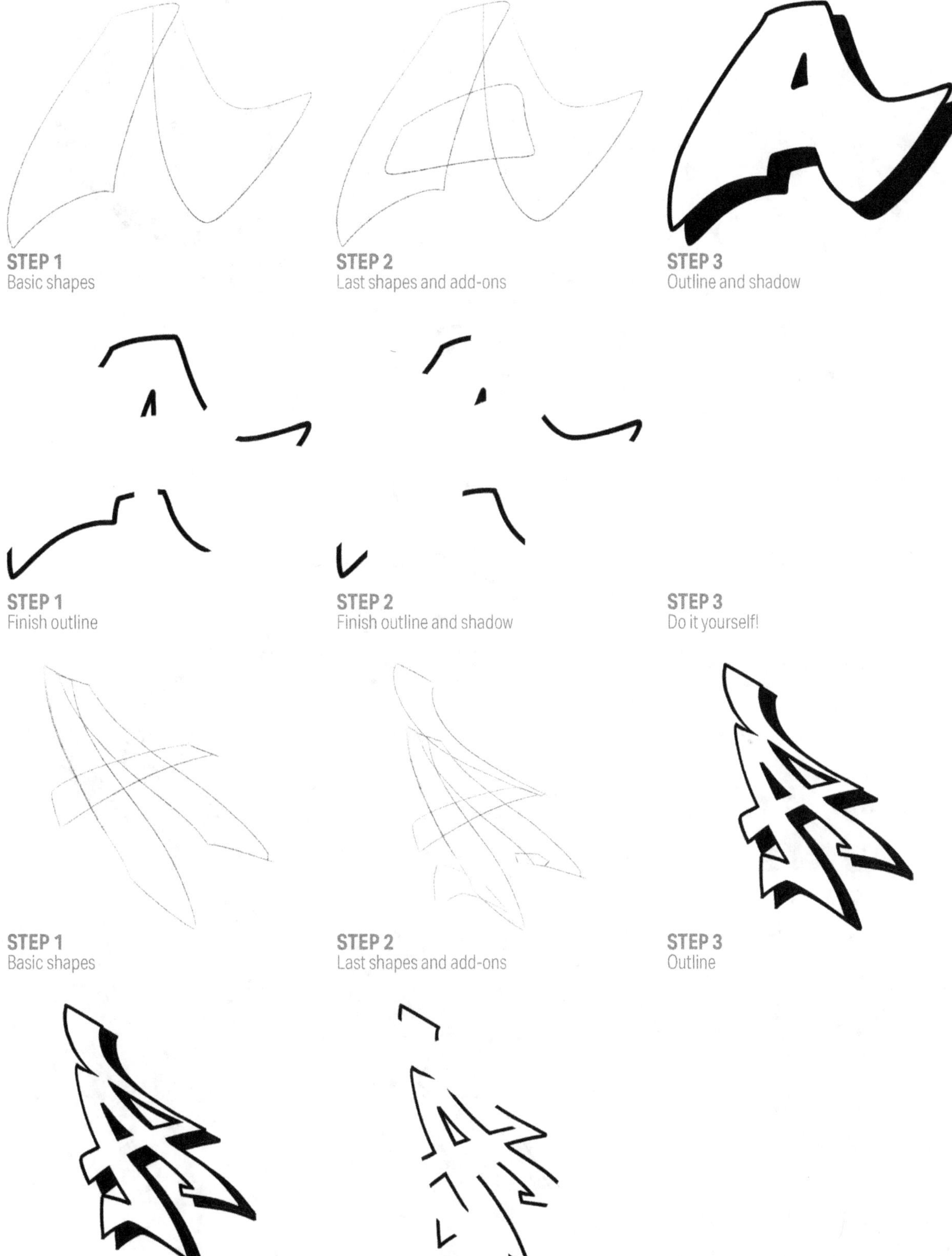

STEP 1
Basic shapes

STEP 2
Last shapes and add-ons

STEP 3
Outline and shadow

STEP 1
Finish outline

STEP 2
Finish outline and shadow

STEP 3
Do it yourself!

STEP 1
Basic shapes

STEP 2
Last shapes and add-ons

STEP 3
Outline

STEP 1
Finish outline

STEP 2
Finish outline

STEP 3
Do it yourself!

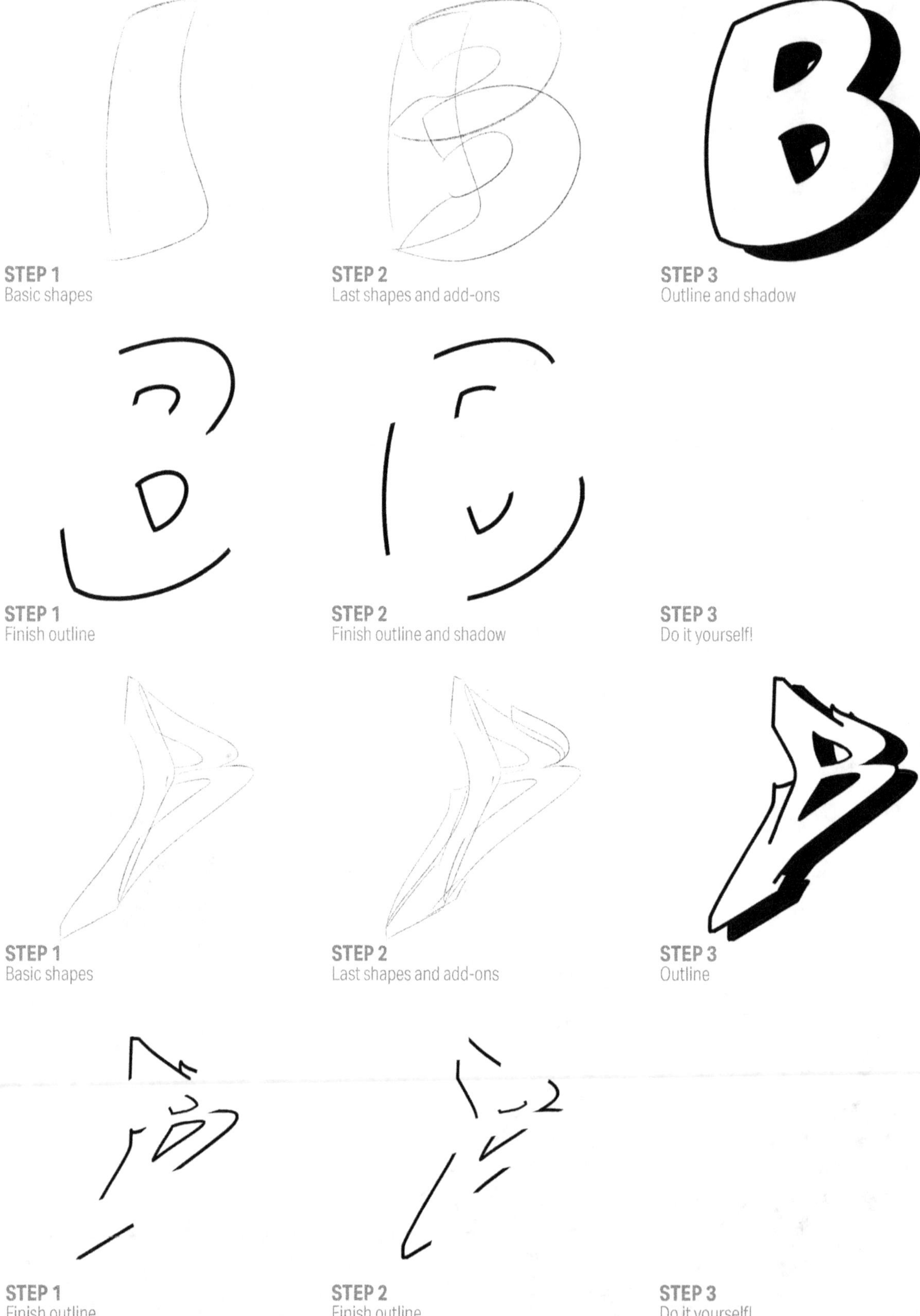

STEP 1
Basic shapes

STEP 2
Last shapes and add-ons

STEP 3
Outline and shadow

STEP 1
Finish outline

STEP 2
Finish outline and shadow

STEP 3
Do it yourself!

STEP 1
Basic shapes

STEP 2
Last shapes and add-ons

STEP 3
Outline

STEP 1
Finish outline

STEP 2
Finish outline

STEP 3
Do it yourself!

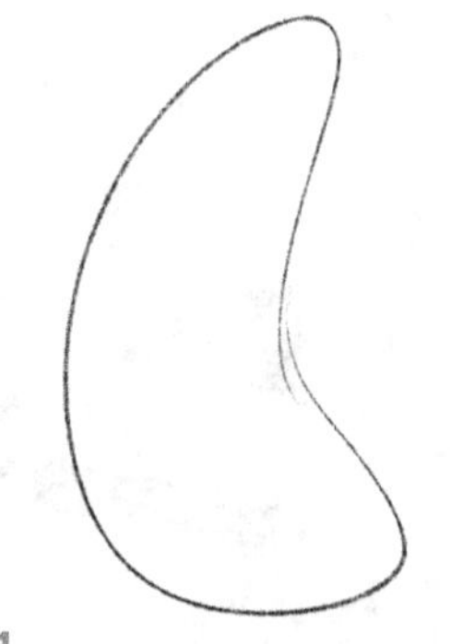

STEP 1
Basic shapes

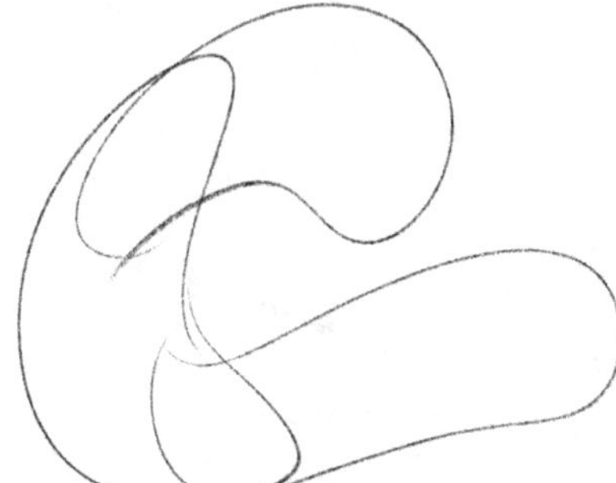

STEP 2
Last shapes and add-ons

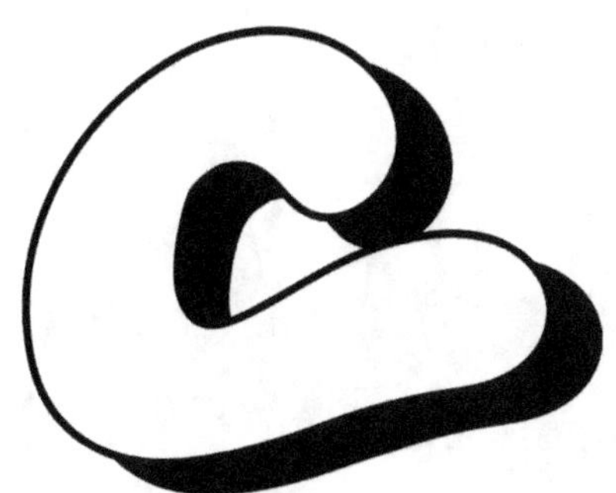

STEP 3
Outline and shadow

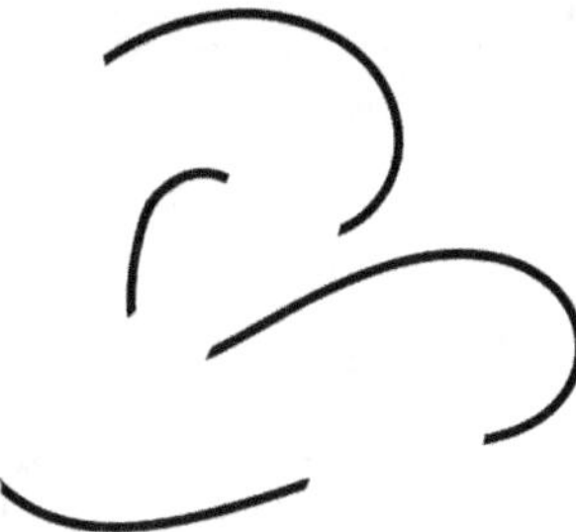

STEP 1
Finish outline

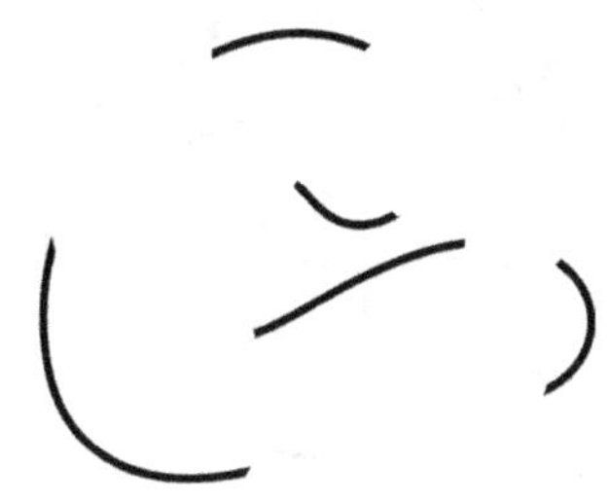

STEP 2
Finish outline and shadow

STEP 3
Do it yourself!

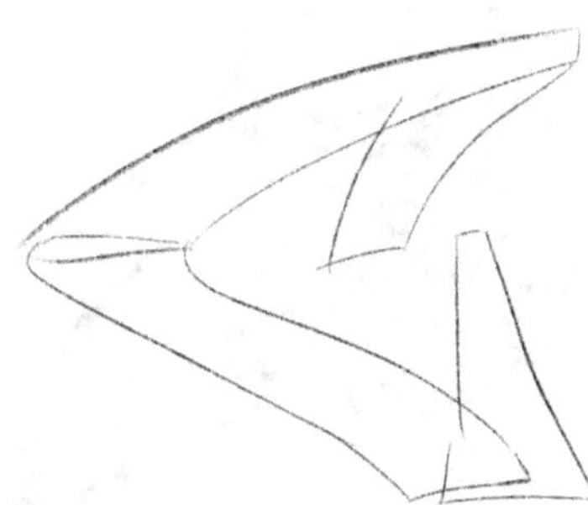

STEP 1
Basic shapes

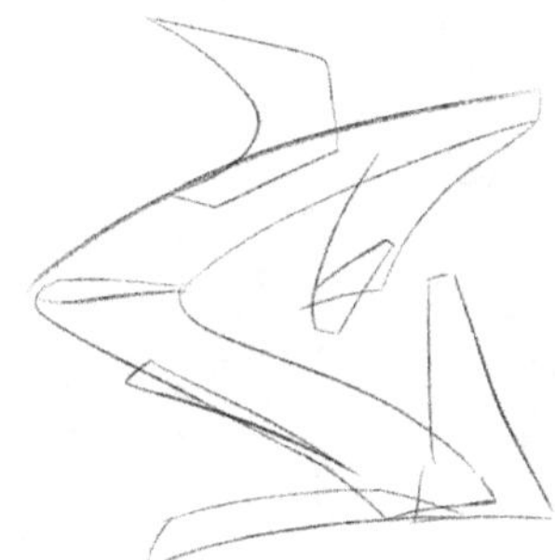

STEP 2
Last shapes and add-ons

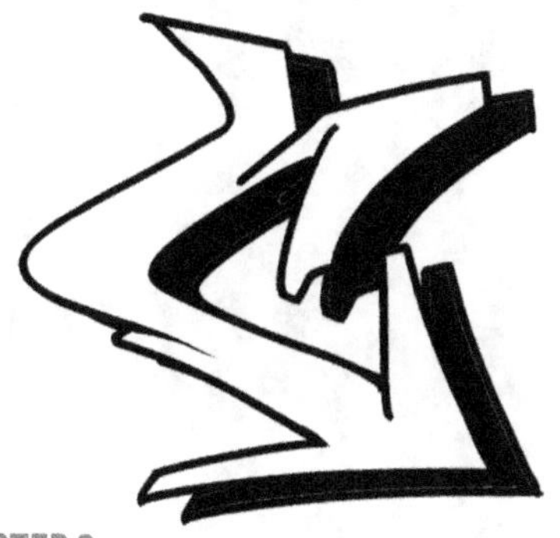

STEP 3
Outline

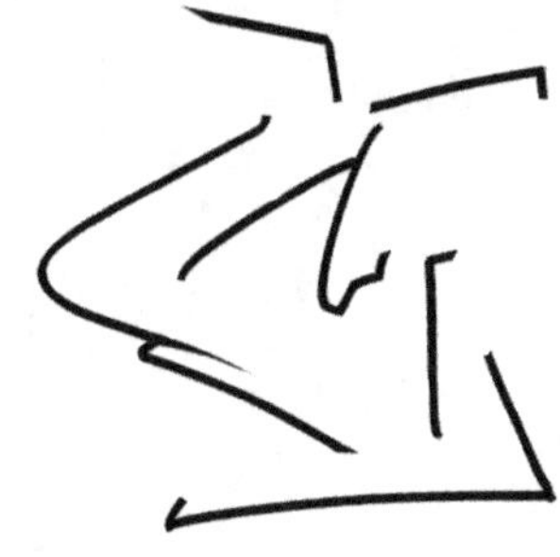

STEP 1
Finish outline

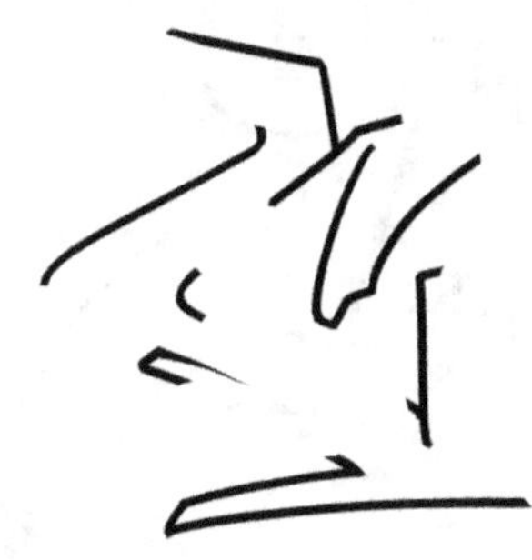

STEP 2
Finish outline

STEP 3
Do it yourself!

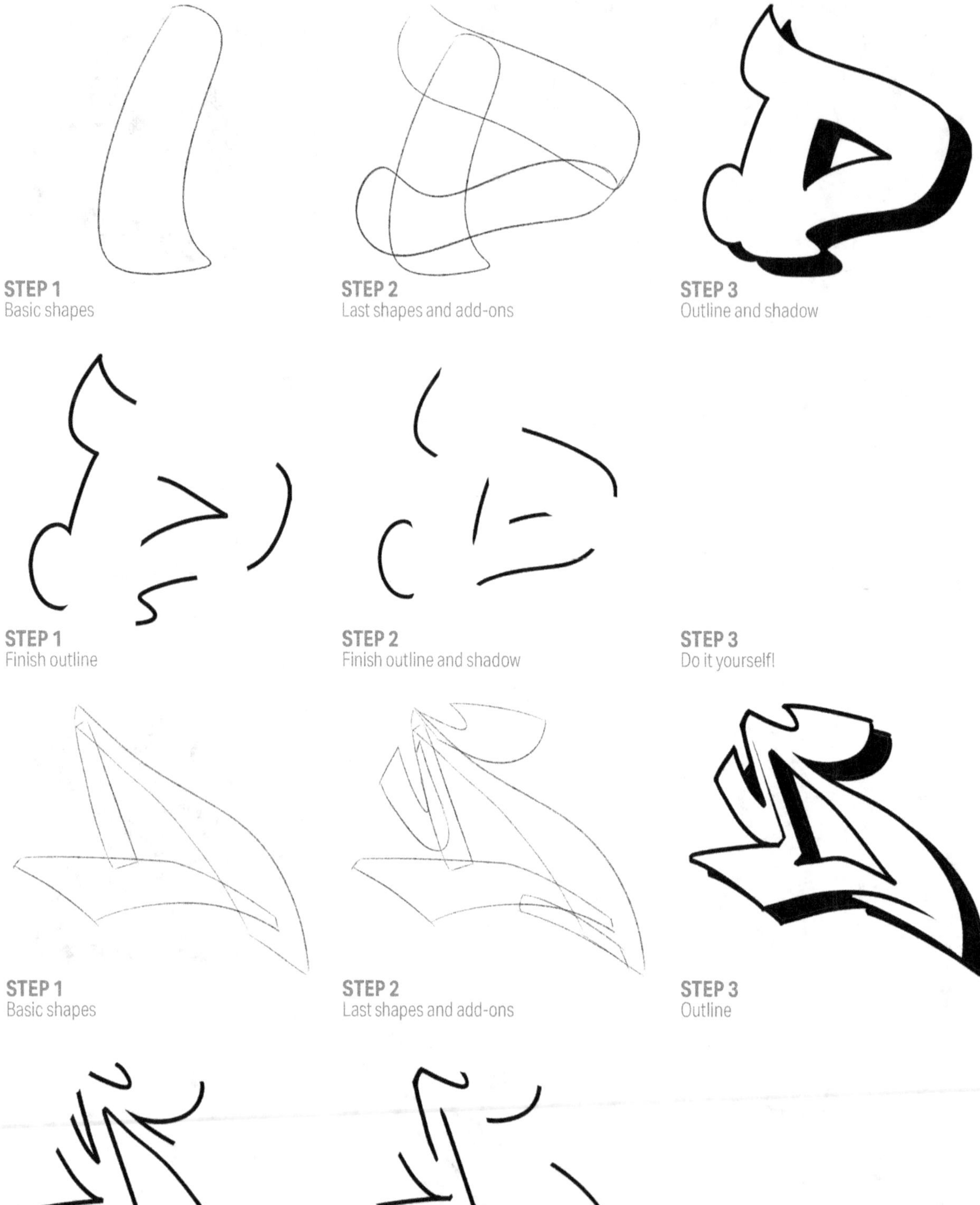

STEP 1
Basic shapes
STEP 2
Last shapes and add-ons
STEP 3
Outline and shadow
STEP 1
Finish outline
STEP 2
Finish outline and shadow
STEP 3
Do it yourself!
STEP 1
Basic shapes
STEP 2
Last shapes and add-ons
STEP 3
Outline
STEP 1
Finish outline
STEP 2
Finish outline
STEP 3
Do it yourself!

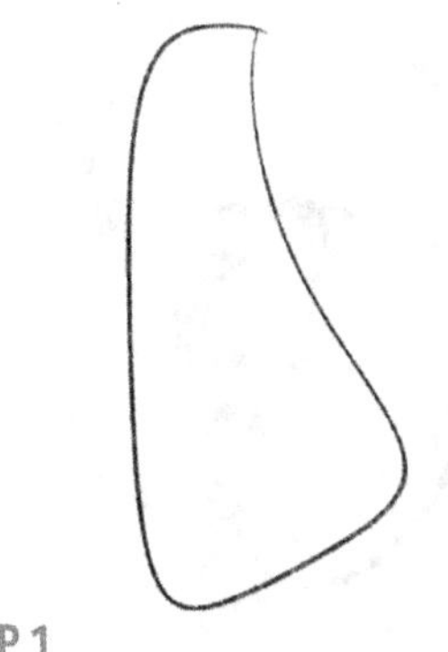

STEP 1
Basic shapes

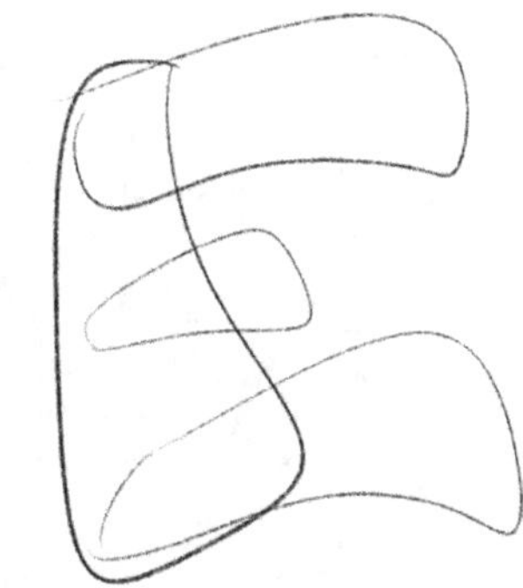

STEP 2
Last shapes and add-ons

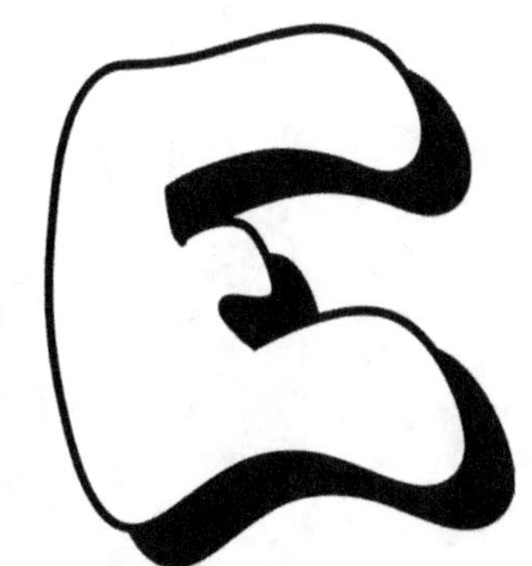

STEP 3
Outline and shadow

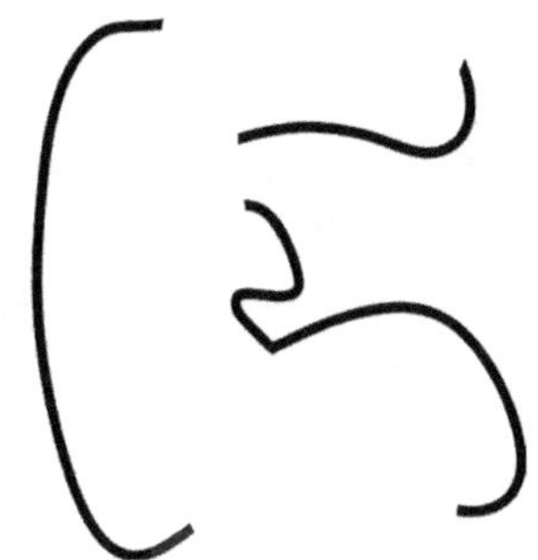

STEP 1
Finish outline

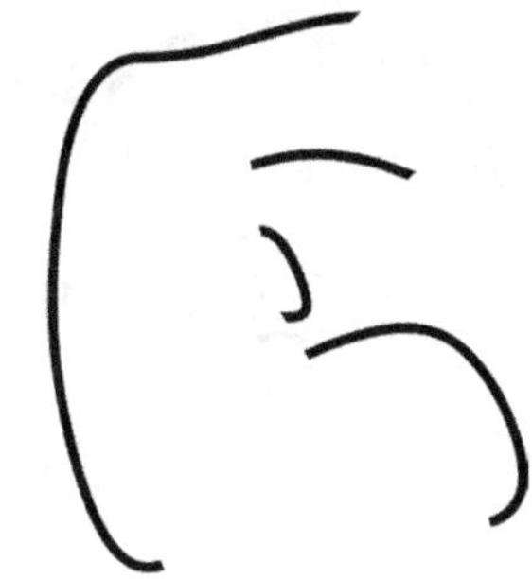

STEP 2
Finish outline and shadow

STEP 3
Do it yourself!

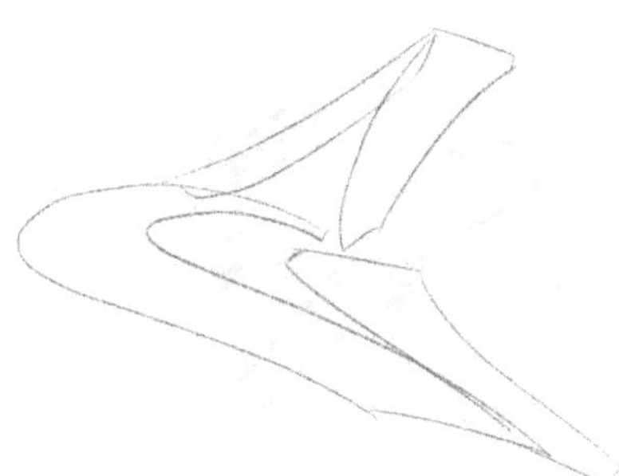

STEP 1
Basic shapes

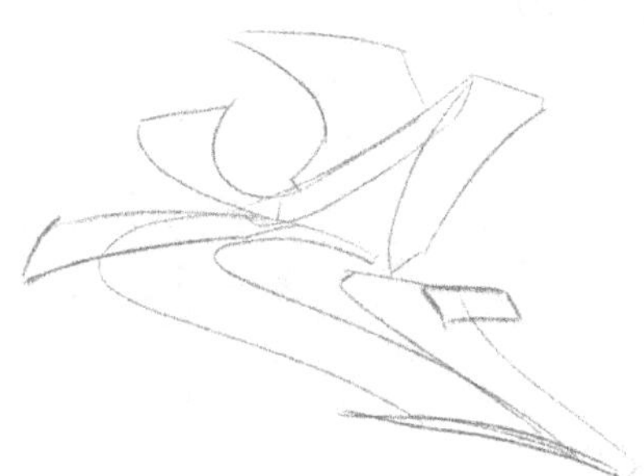

STEP 2
Last shapes and add-ons

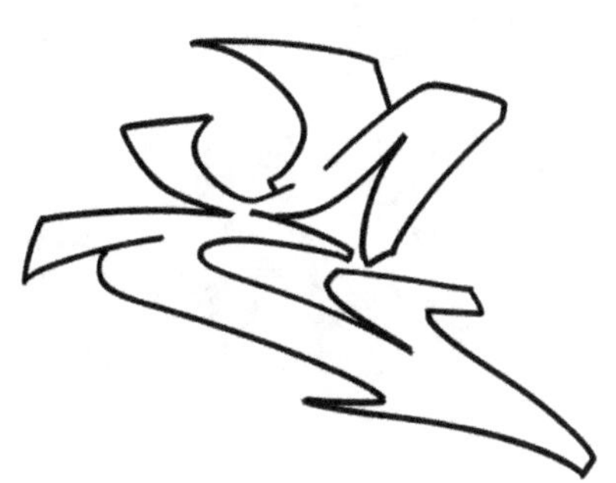

STEP 3
Outline

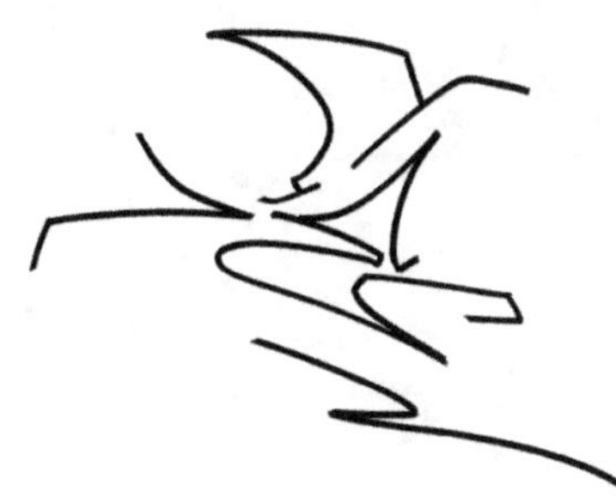

STEP 1
Finish outline

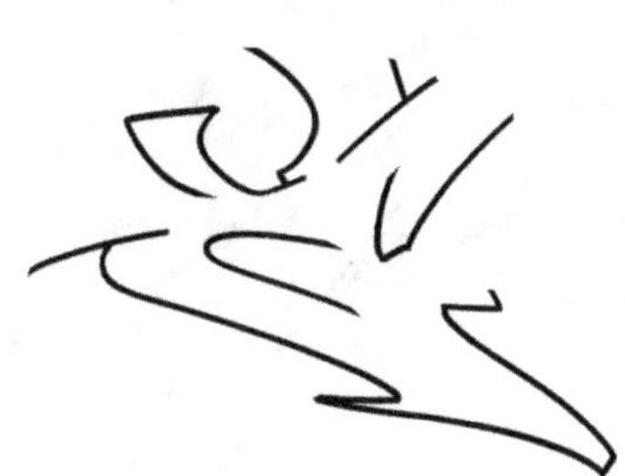

STEP 2
Finish outline

STEP 3
Do it yourself!

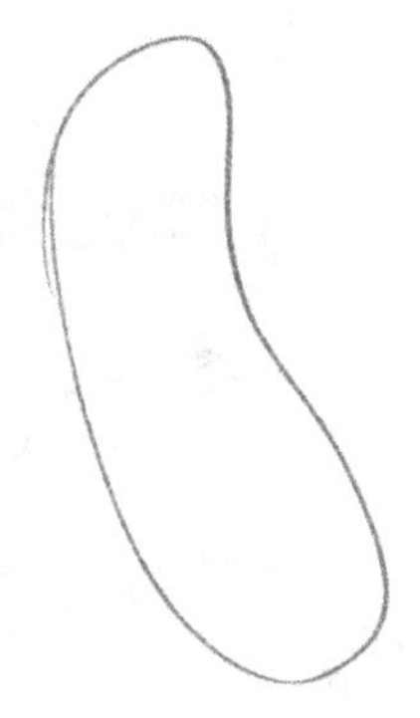

STEP 1
Basic shapes

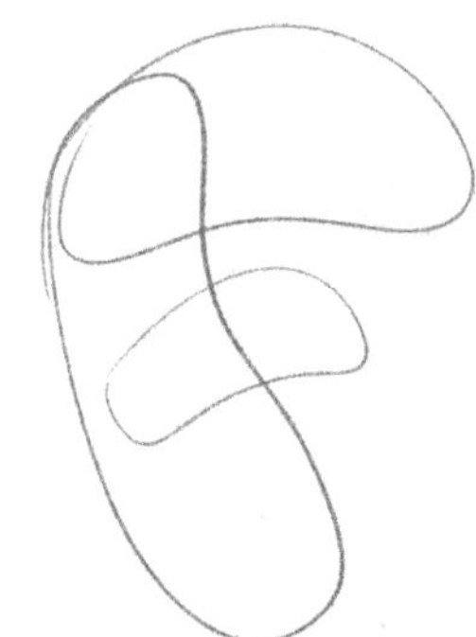

STEP 2
Last shapes and add-ons

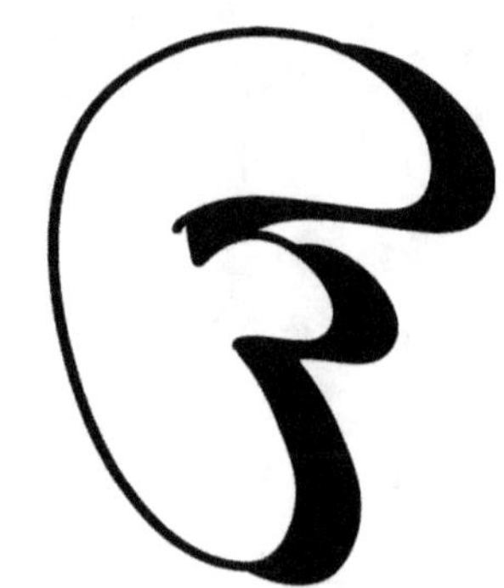

STEP 3
Outline and shadow

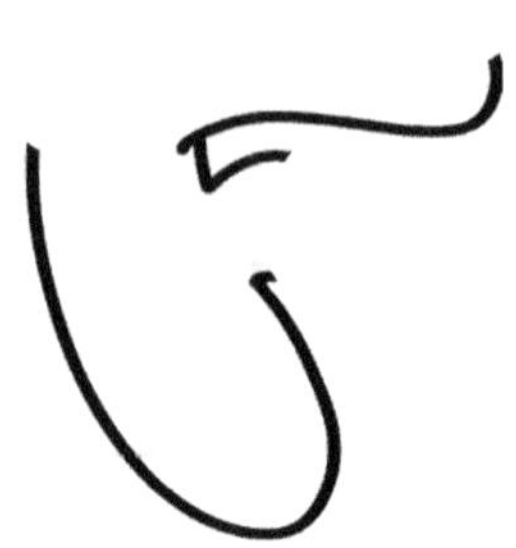

STEP 1
Finish outline

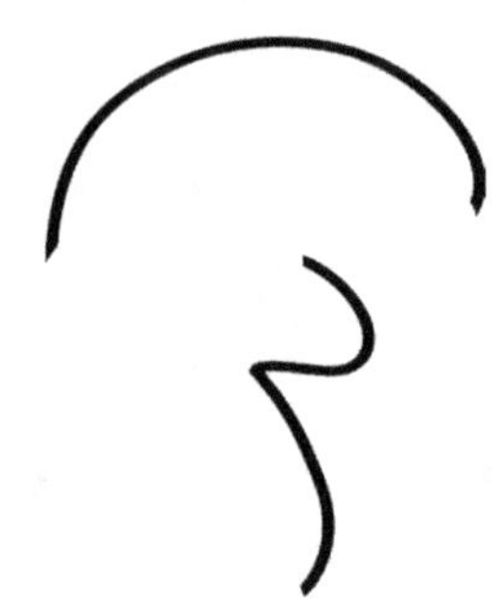

STEP 2
Finish outline and shadow

STEP 3
Do it yourself!

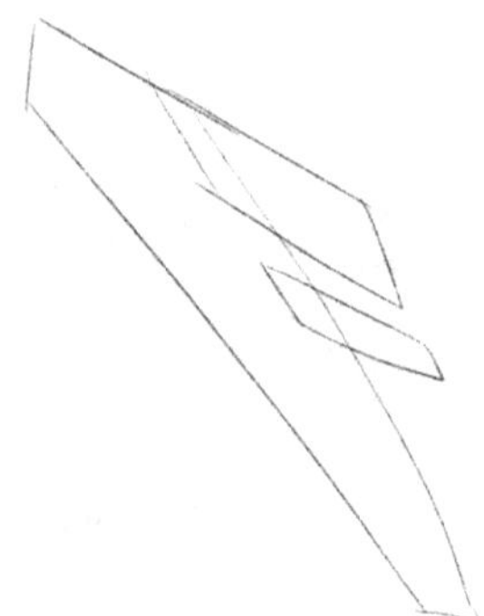

STEP 1
Basic shapes

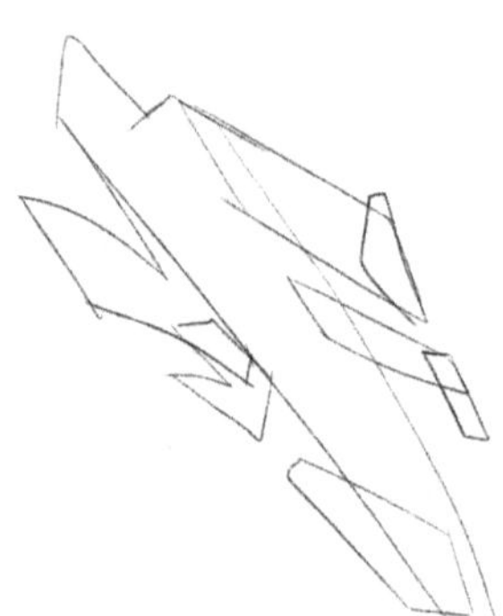

STEP 2
Last shapes and add-ons

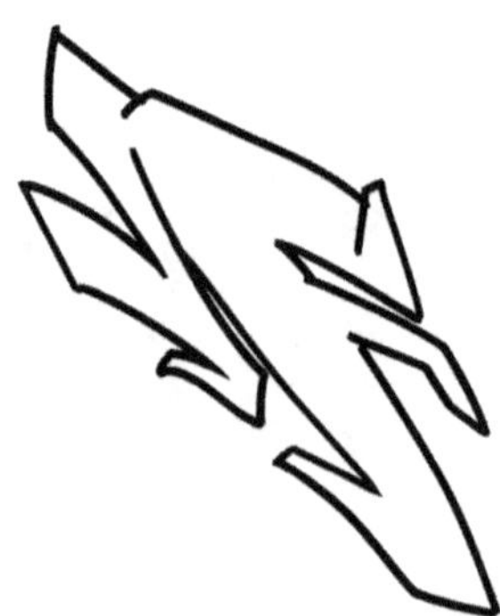

STEP 3
Outline

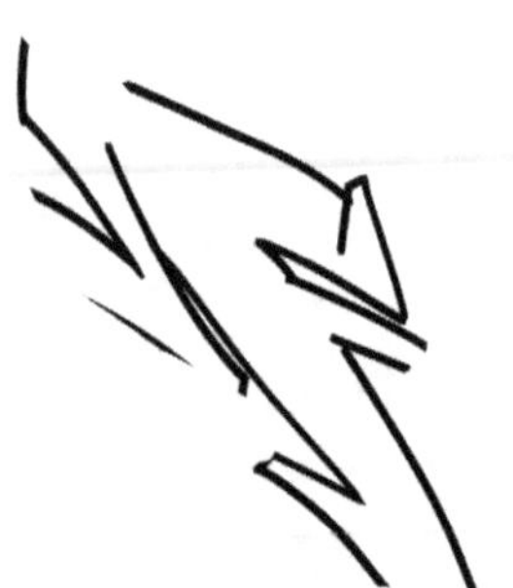

STEP 1
Finish outline

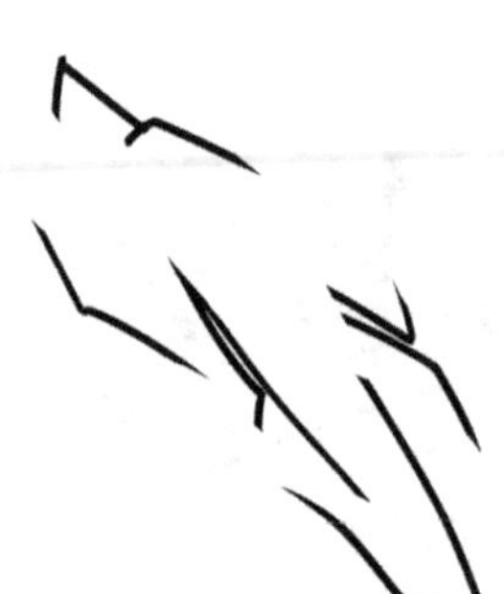

STEP 2
Finish outline

STEP 3
Do it yourself!

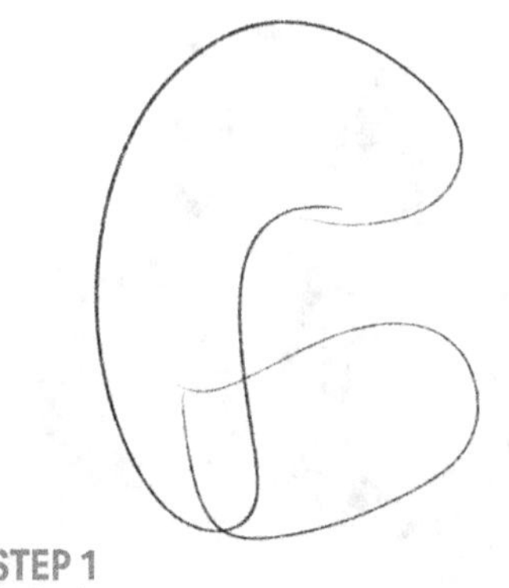

STEP 1
Basic shapes

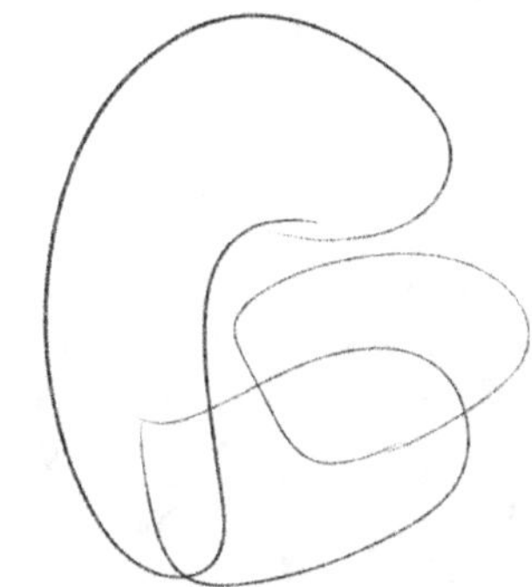

STEP 2
Last shapes and add-ons

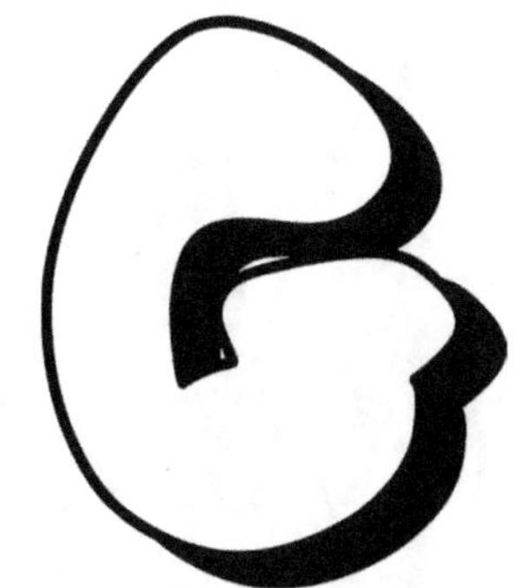

STEP 3
Outline and shadow

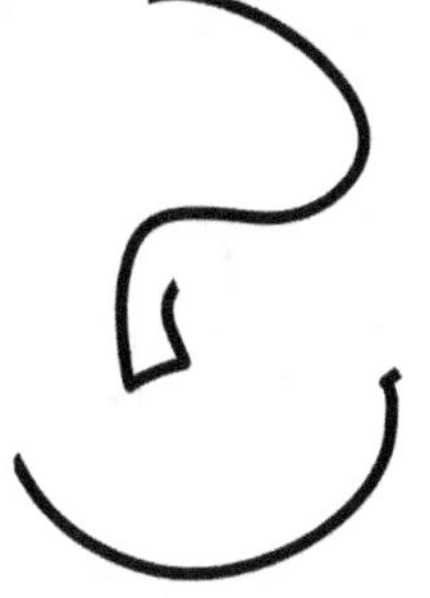

STEP 1
Finish outline

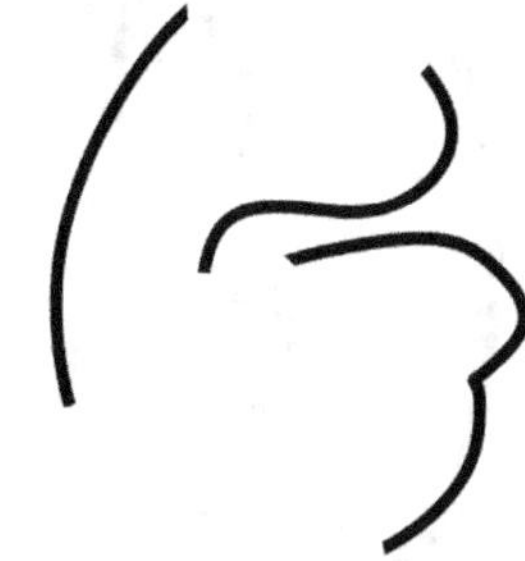

STEP 2
Finish outline and shadow

STEP 3
Do it yourself!

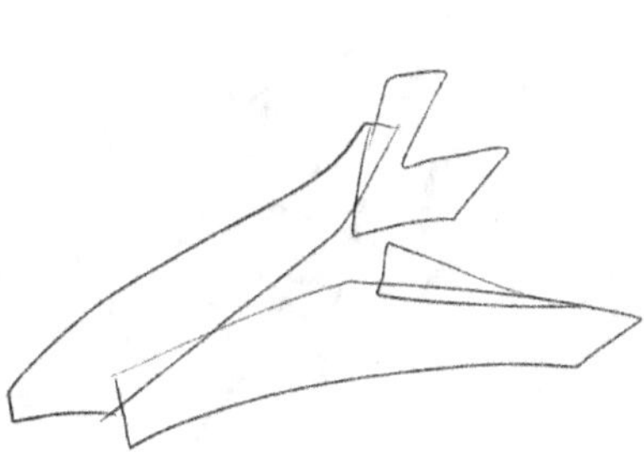

STEP 1
Basic shapes

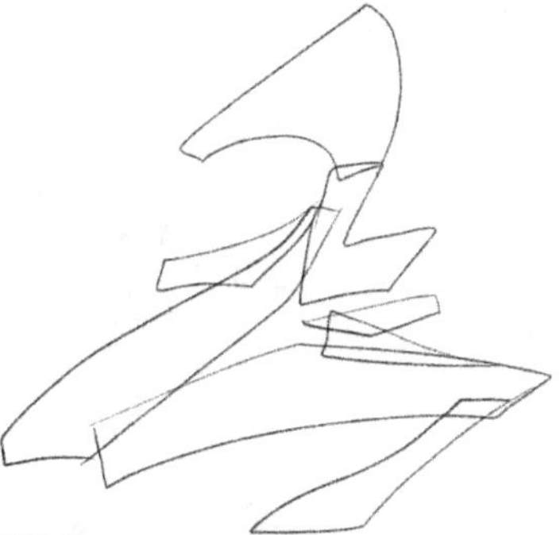

STEP 2
Last shapes and add-ons

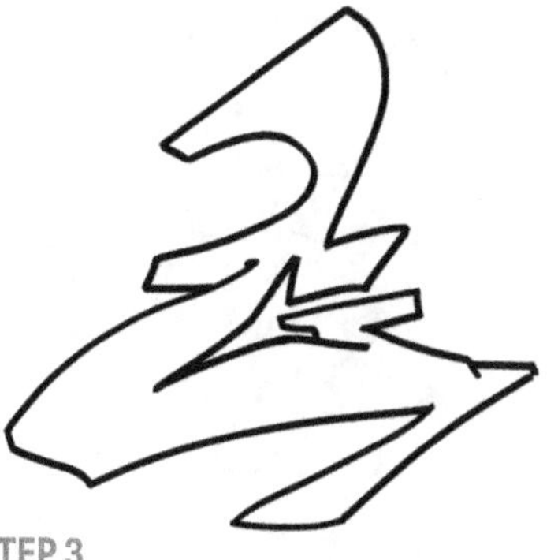

STEP 3
Outline

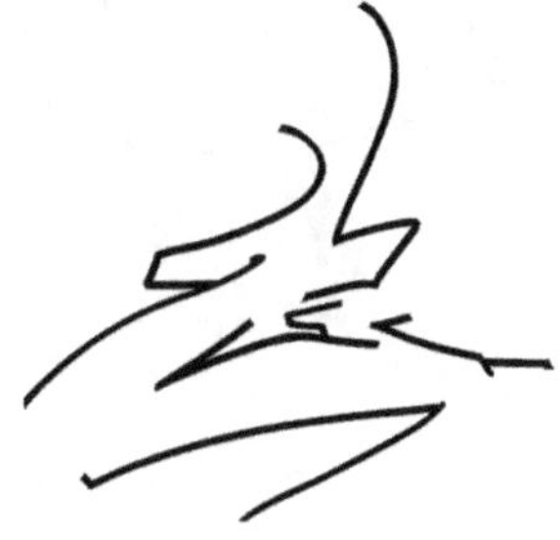

STEP 1
Finish outline

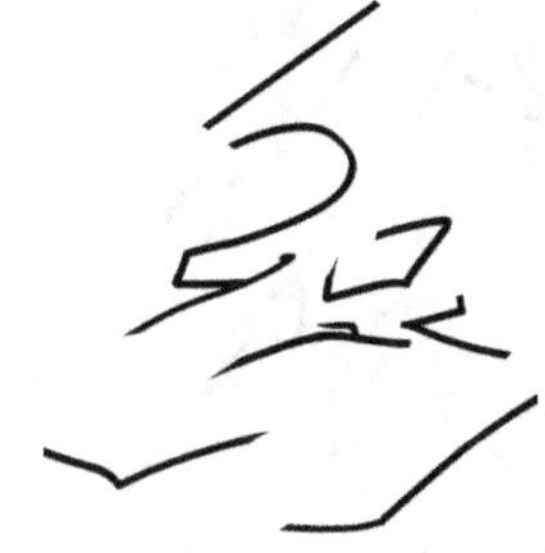

STEP 2
Finish outline

STEP 3
Do it yourself!

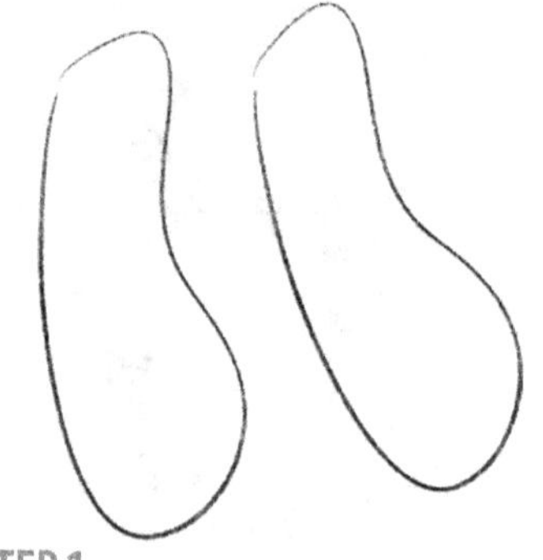

STEP 1
Basic shapes

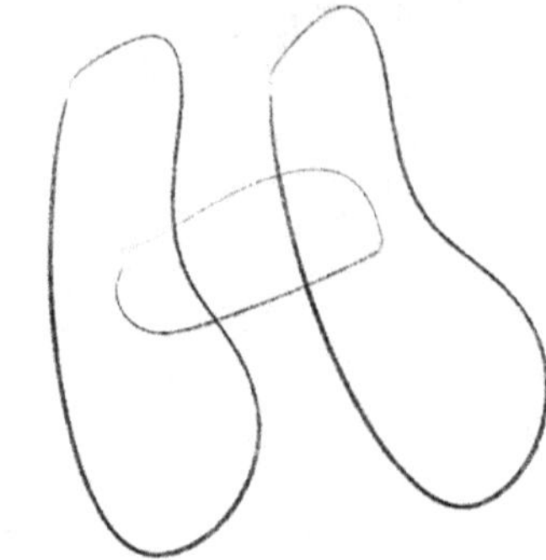

STEP 2
Last shapes and add-ons

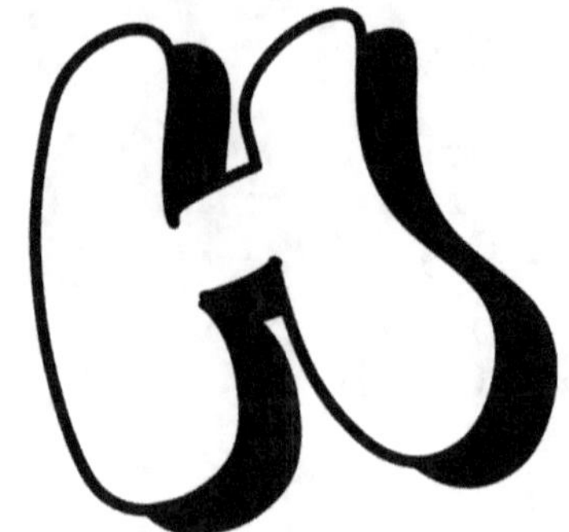

STEP 3
Outline and shadow

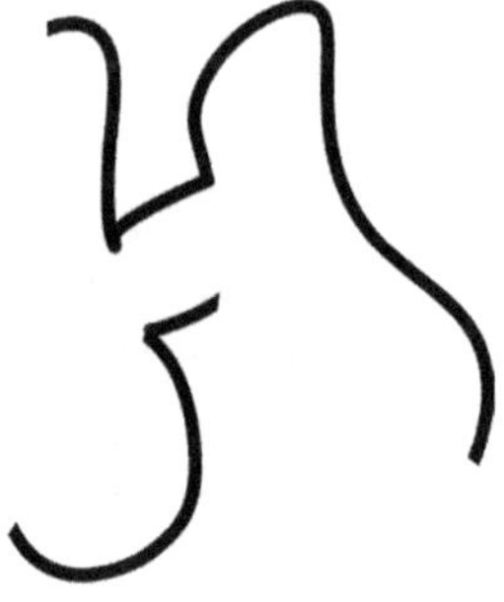

STEP 1
Finish outline

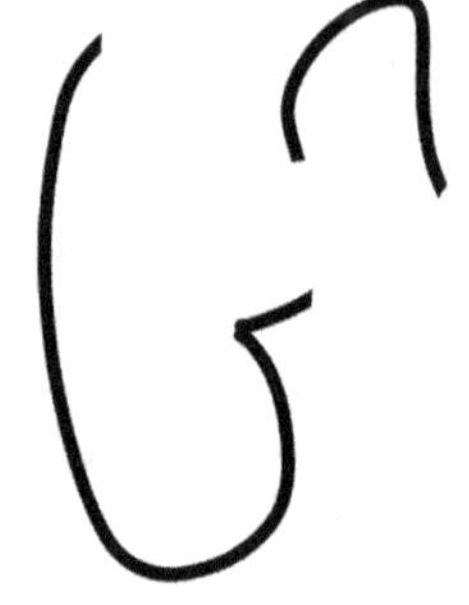
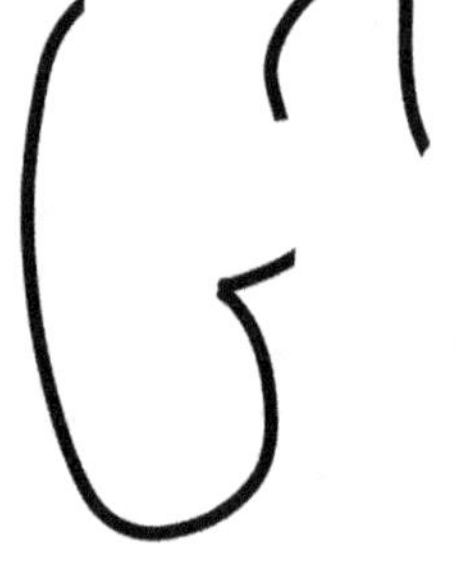

STEP 2
Finish outline and shadow

STEP 3
Do it yourself!

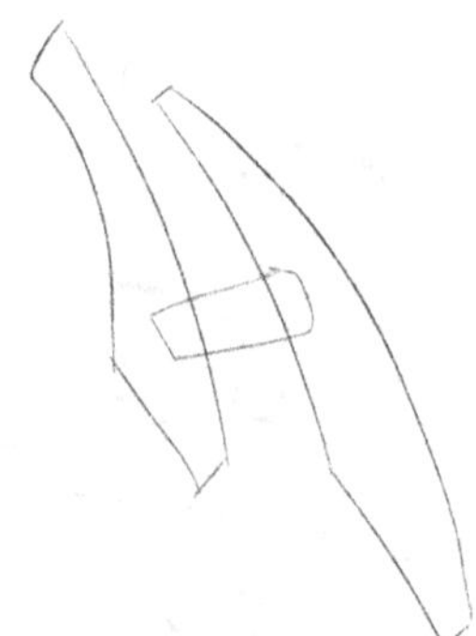

STEP 1
Basic shapes

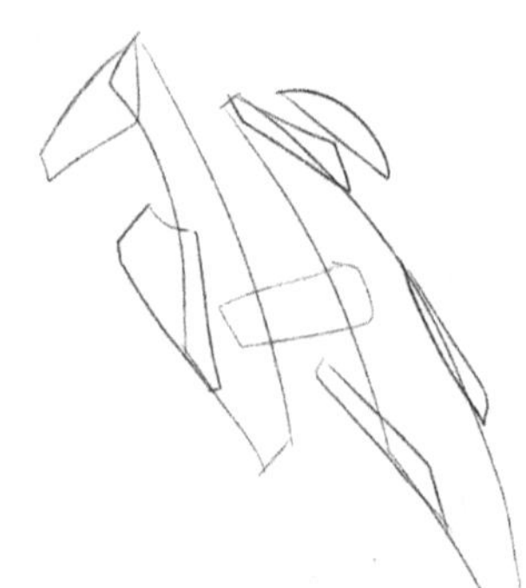

STEP 2
Last shapes and add-ons

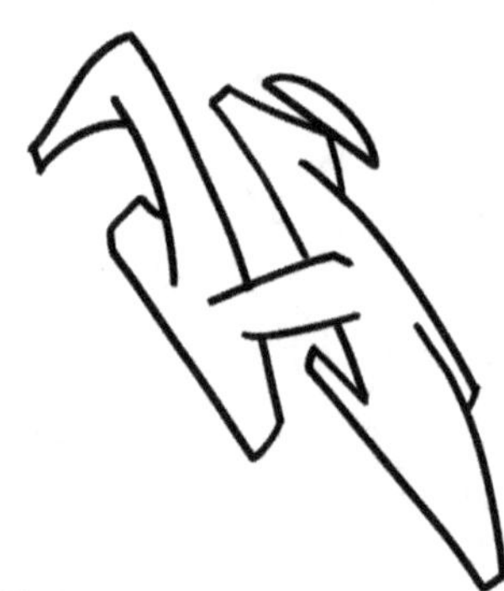

STEP 3
Outline

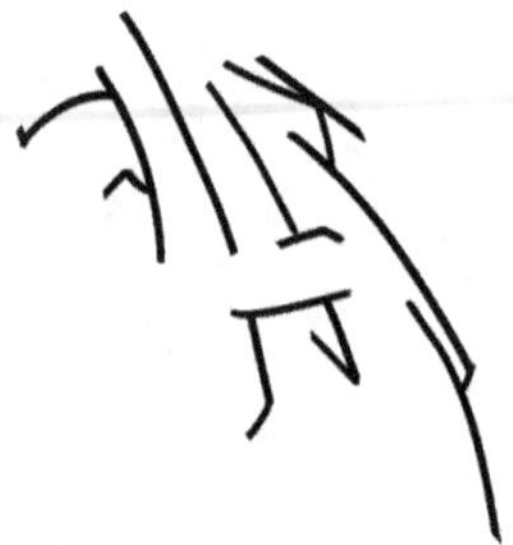

STEP 1
Finish outline

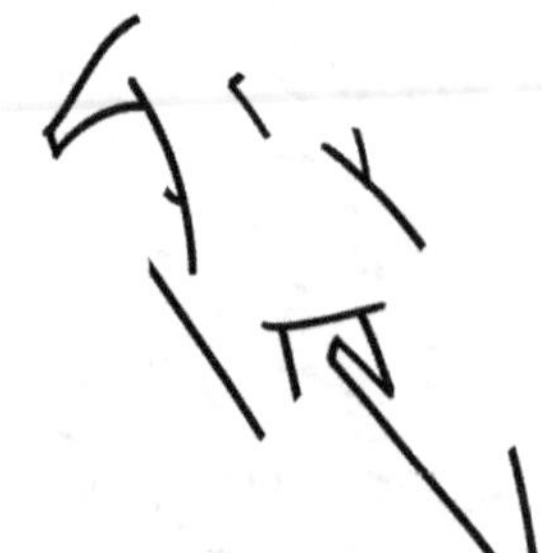

STEP 2
Finish outline

STEP 3
Do it yourself!

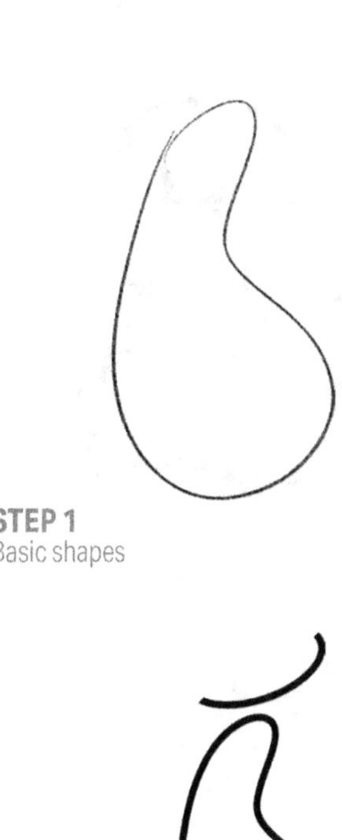

STEP 1
Basic shapes

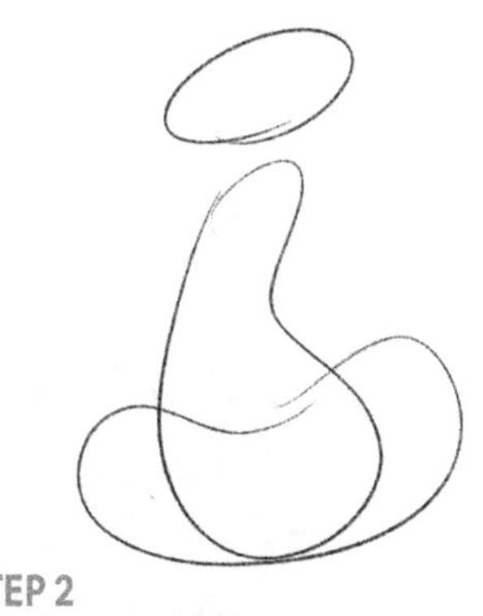

STEP 2
Last shapes and add-ons

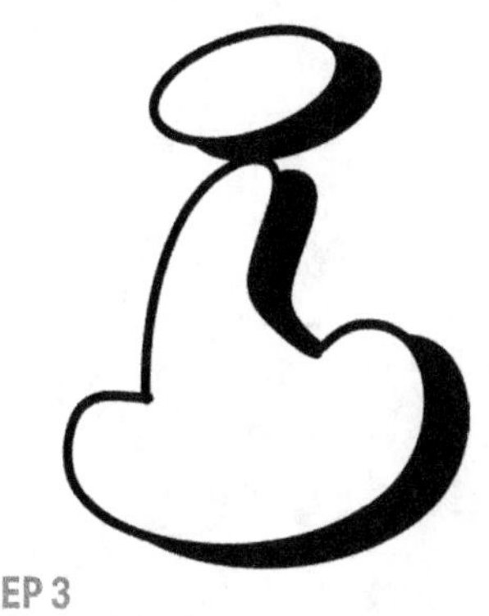

STEP 3
Outline and shadow

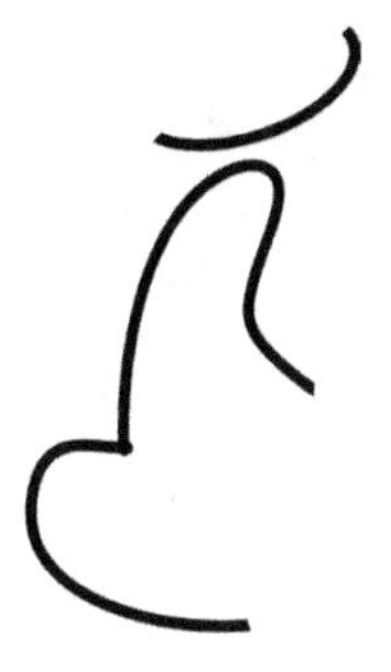

STEP 1
Finish outline

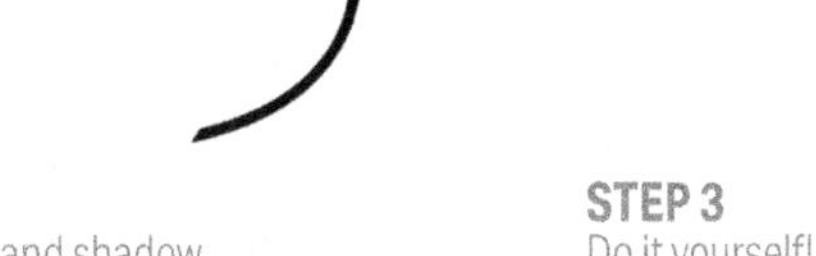

STEP 2
Finish outline and shadow

STEP 3
Do it yourself!

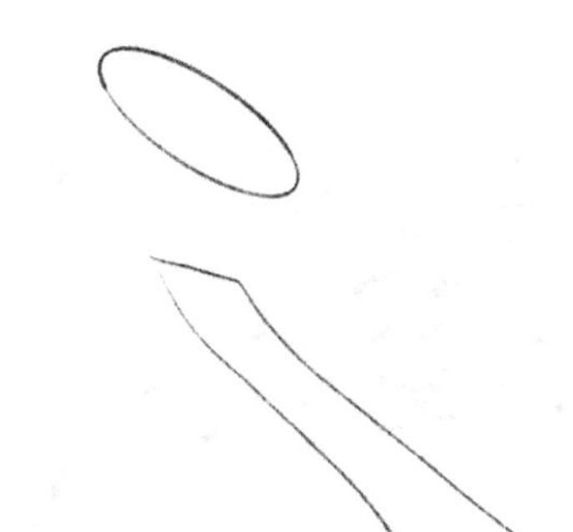

STEP 1
Basic shapes

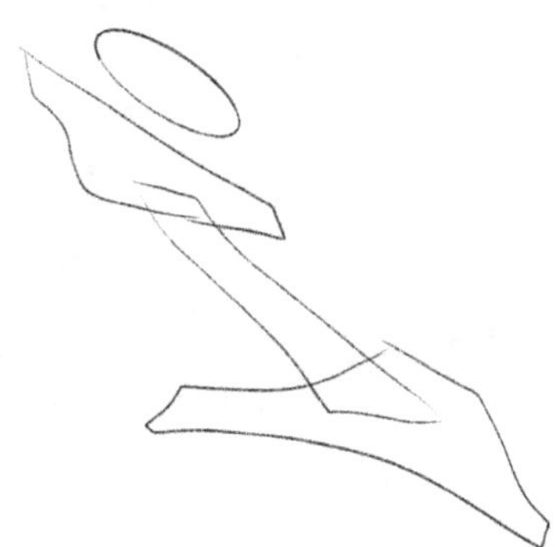

STEP 2
Last shapes and add-ons

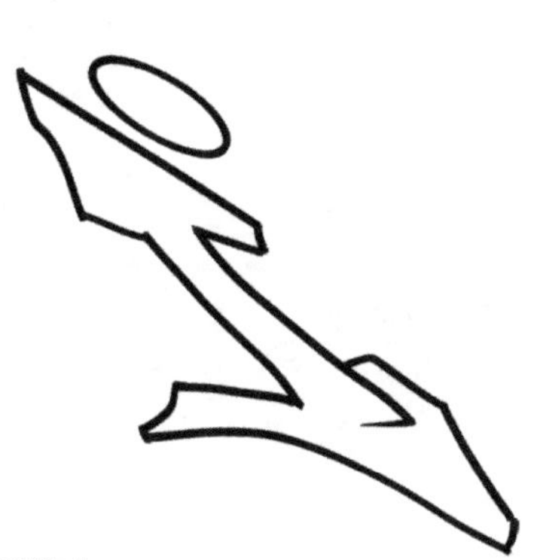

STEP 3
Outline

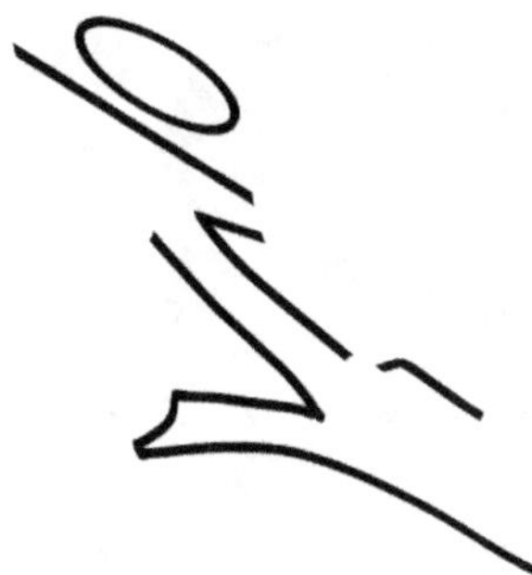

STEP 1
Finish outline

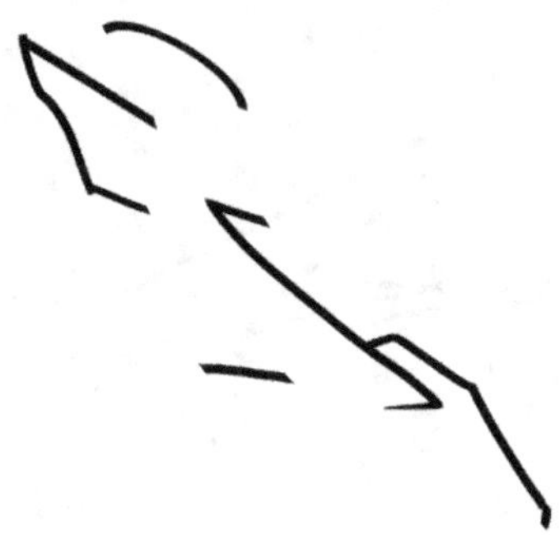

STEP 2
Finish outline

STEP 3
Do it yourself!

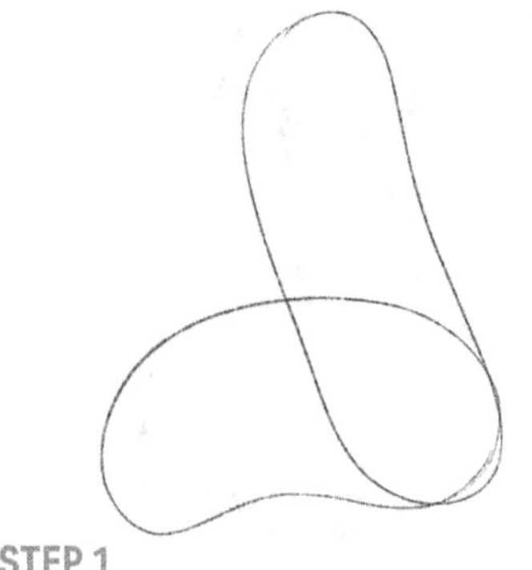

STEP 1
Basic shapes

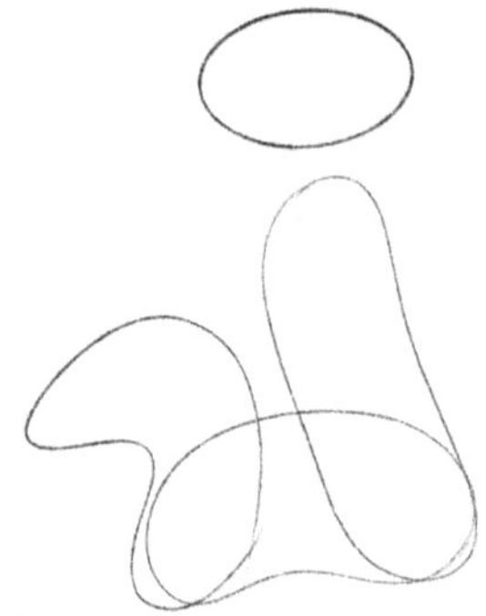

STEP 2
Last shapes and add-ons

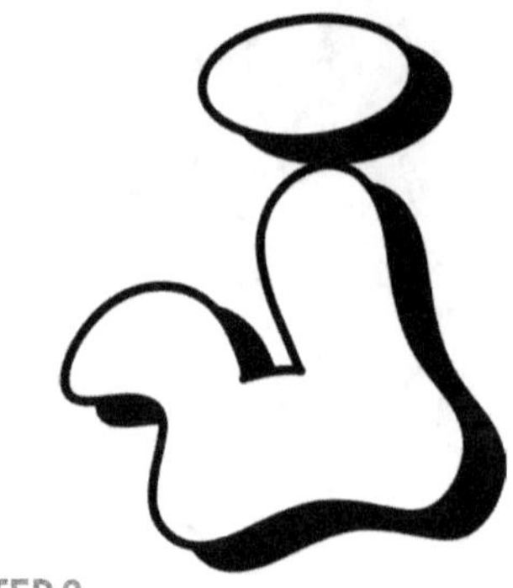

STEP 3
Outline and shadow

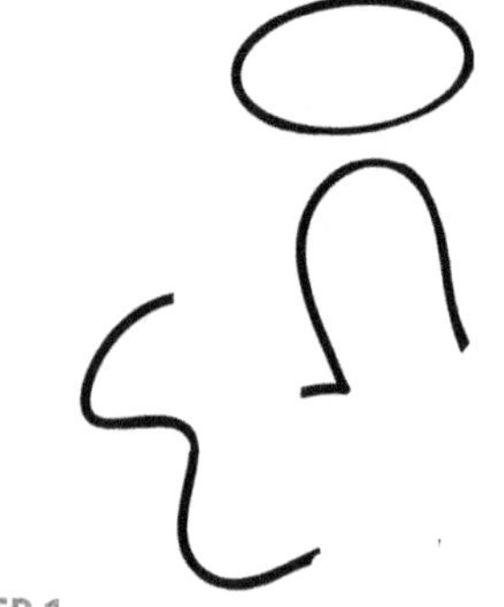

STEP 1
Finish outline

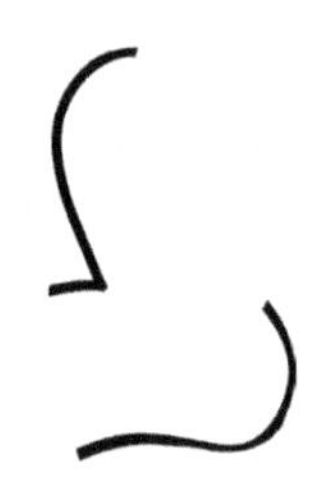

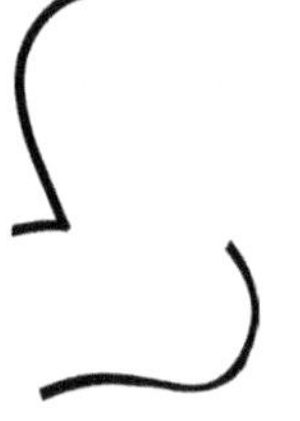

STEP 2
Finish outline and shadow

STEP 3
Do it yourself!

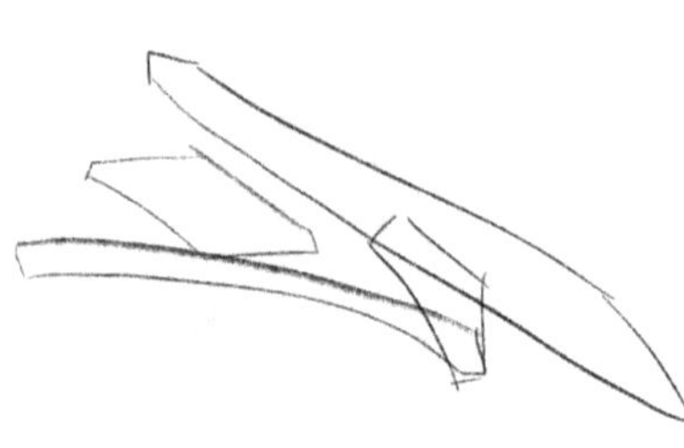

STEP 1
Basic shapes

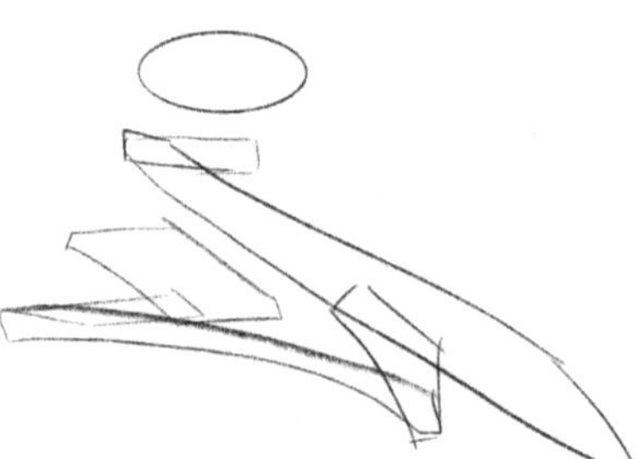

STEP 2
Last shapes and add-ons

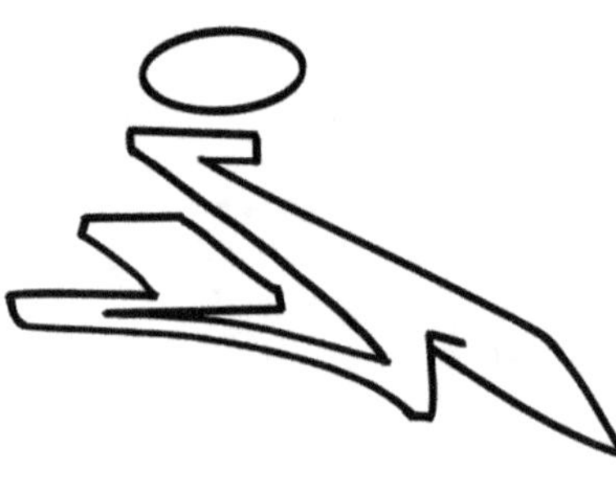

STEP 3
Outline

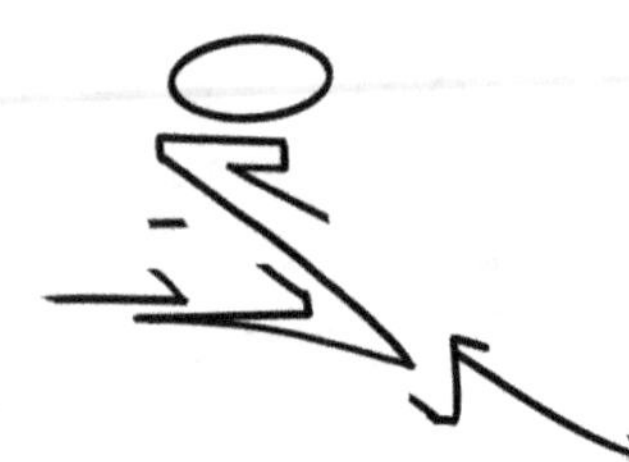

STEP 1
Finish outline

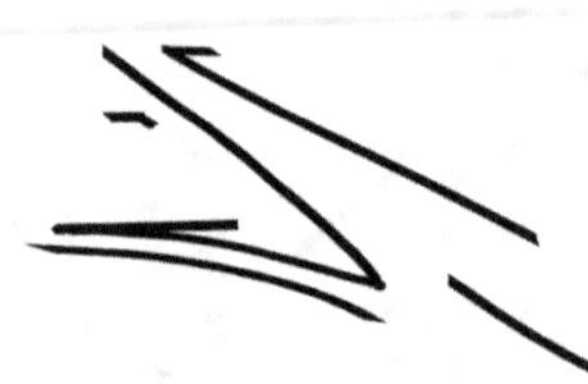

STEP 2
Finish outline

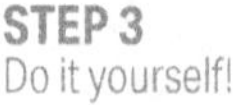

STEP 3
Do it yourself!

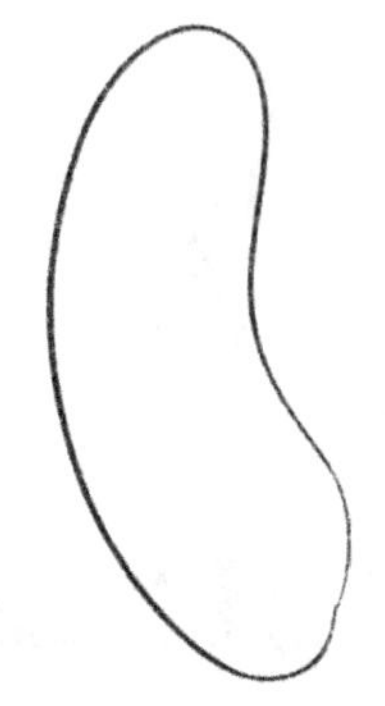

STEP 1
Basic shapes

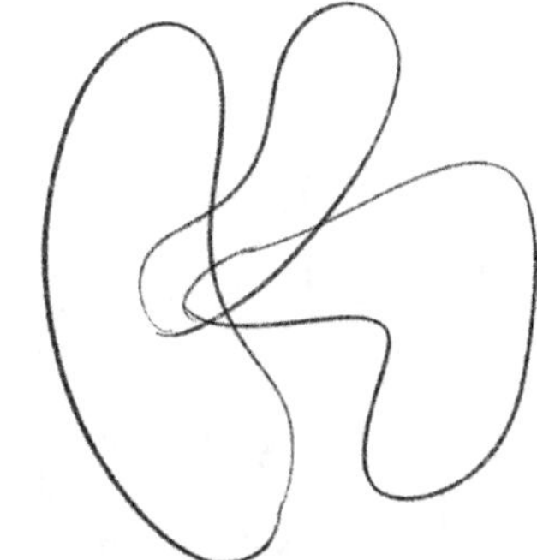

STEP 2
Last shapes and add-ons

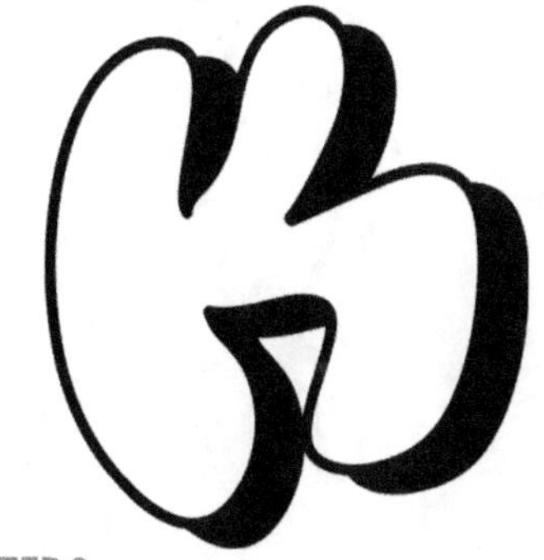

STEP 3
Outline and shadow

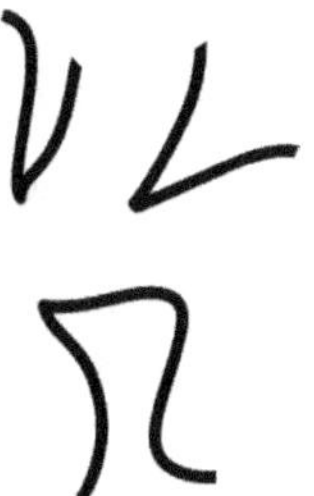

STEP 1
Finish outline

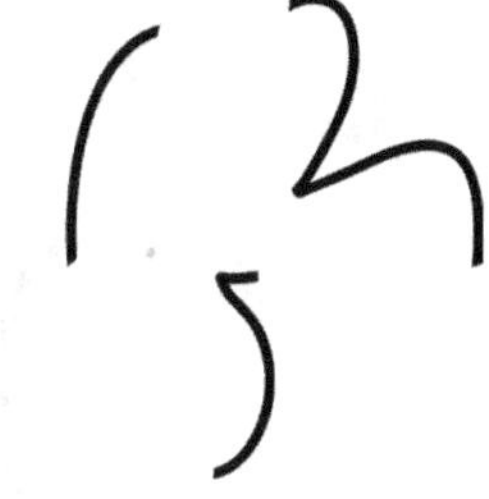
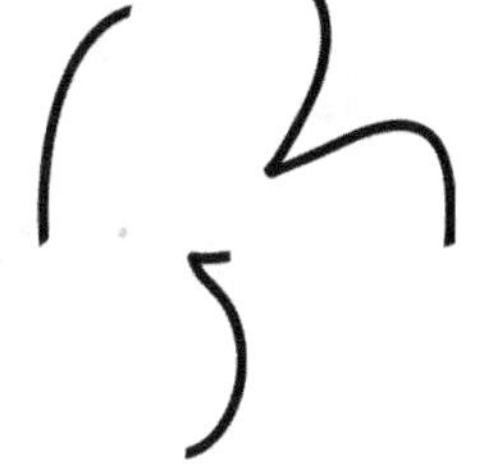

STEP 2
Finish outline and shadow

STEP 3
Do it yourself!

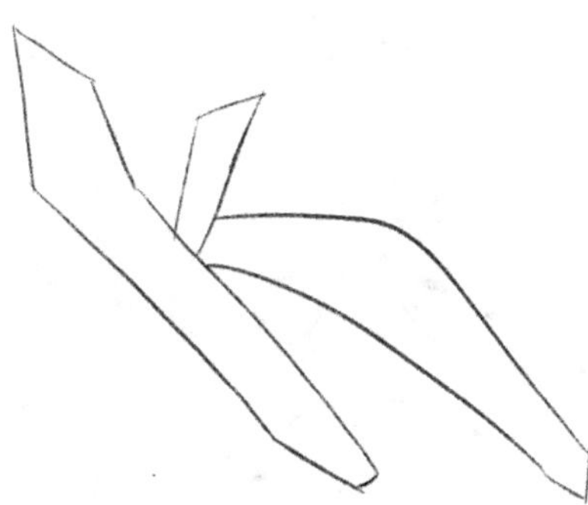

STEP 1
Basic shapes

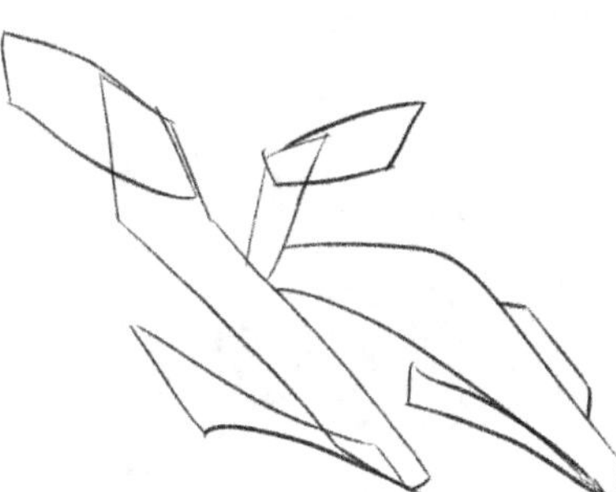

STEP 2
Last shapes and add-ons

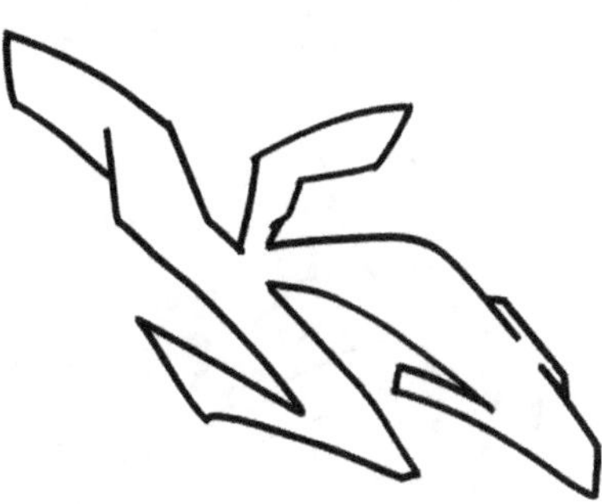

STEP 3
Outline

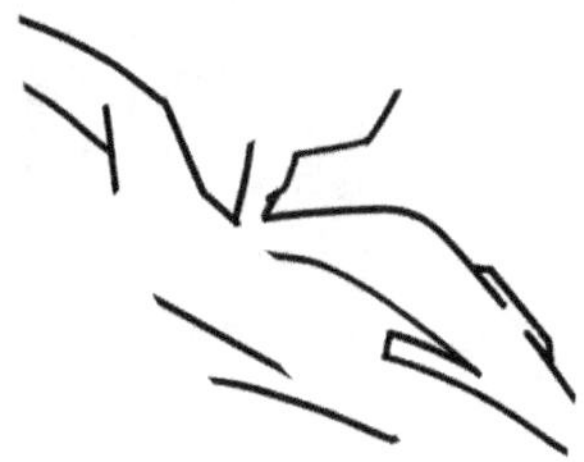

STEP 1
Finish outline

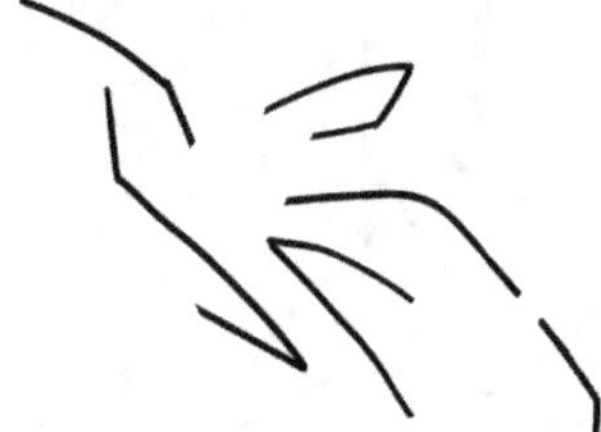

STEP 2
Finish outline

STEP 3
Do it yourself!

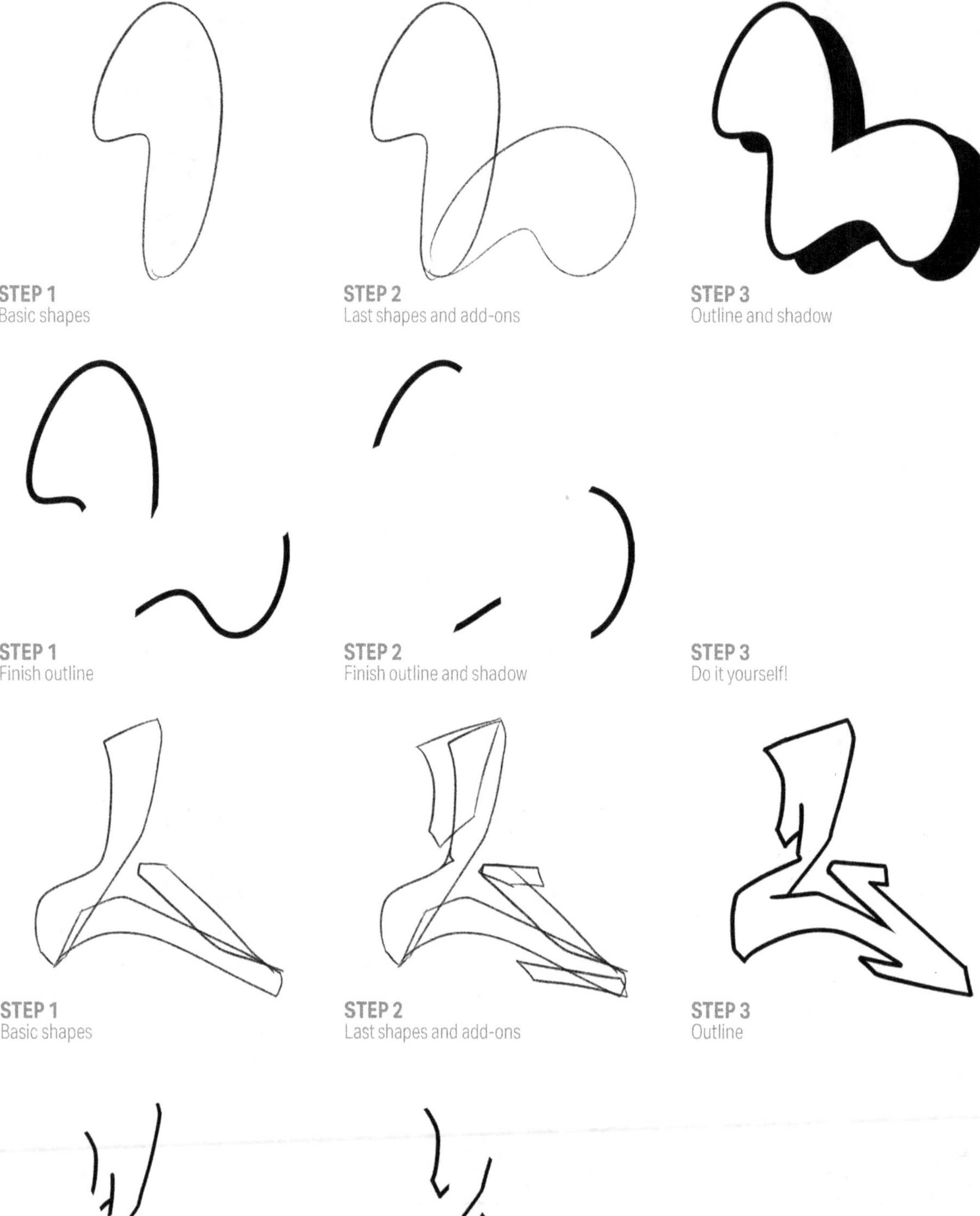

STEP 1
Basic shapes
STEP 2
Last shapes and add-ons
STEP 3
Outline and shadow
STEP 1
Finish outline
STEP 2
Finish outline and shadow
STEP 3
Do it yourself!
STEP 1
Basic shapes
STEP 2
Last shapes and add-ons
STEP 3
Outline
STEP 1
Finish outline
STEP 2
Finish outline
STEP 3
Do it yourself!

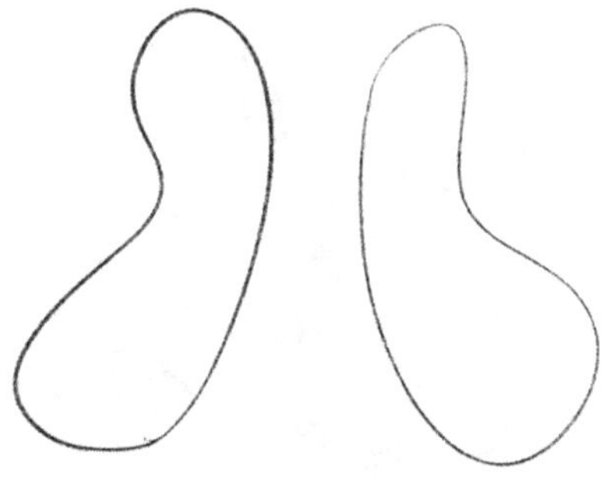

STEP 1
Basic shapes

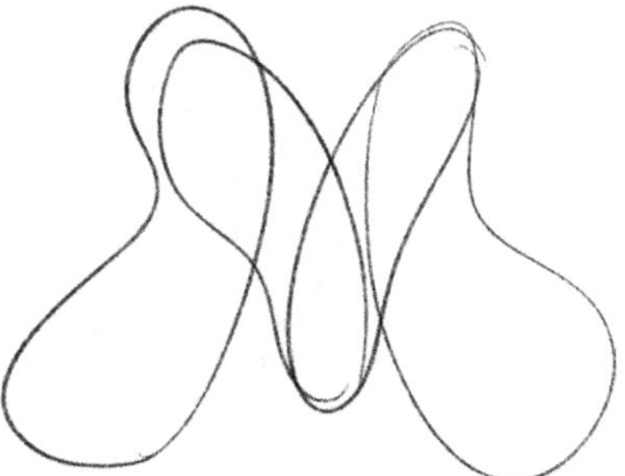

STEP 2
Last shapes and add-ons

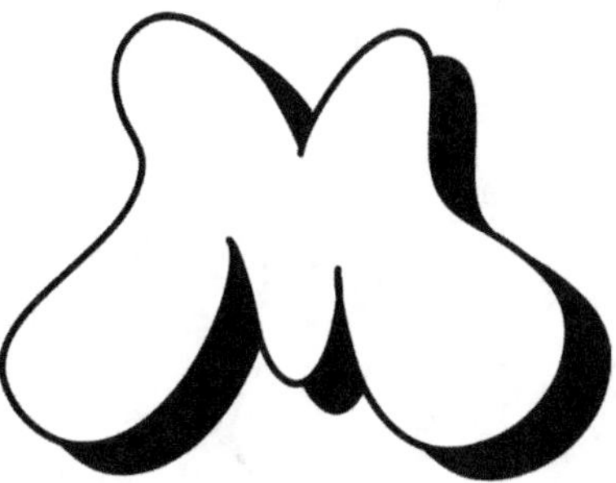

STEP 3
Outline and shadow

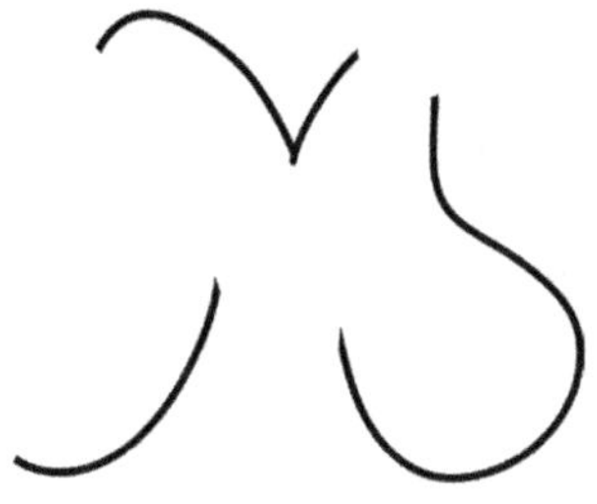

STEP 1
Finish outline

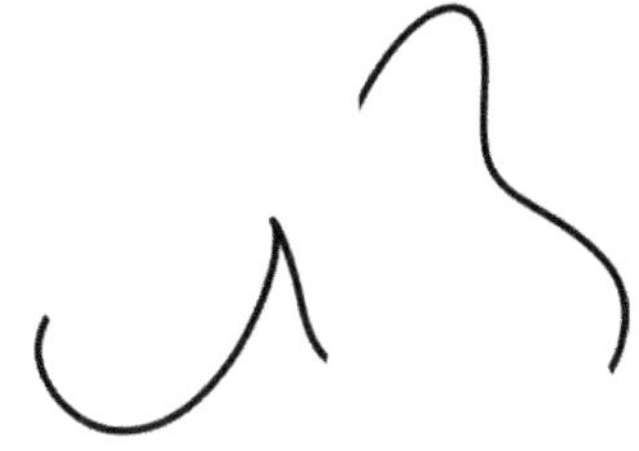
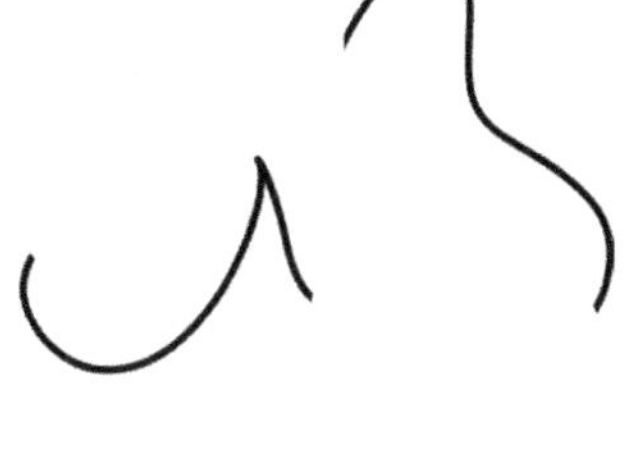

STEP 2
Finish outline and shadow

STEP 3
Do it yourself!

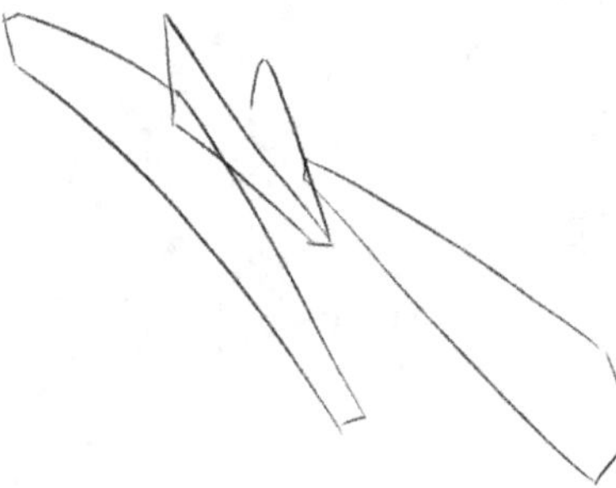

STEP 1
Basic shapes

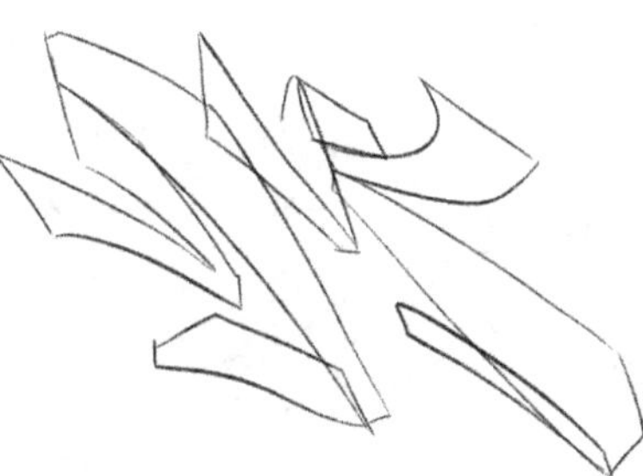

STEP 2
Last shapes and add-ons

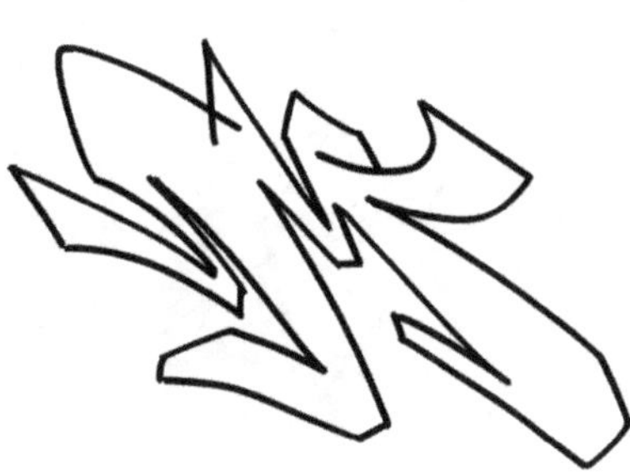

STEP 3
Outline

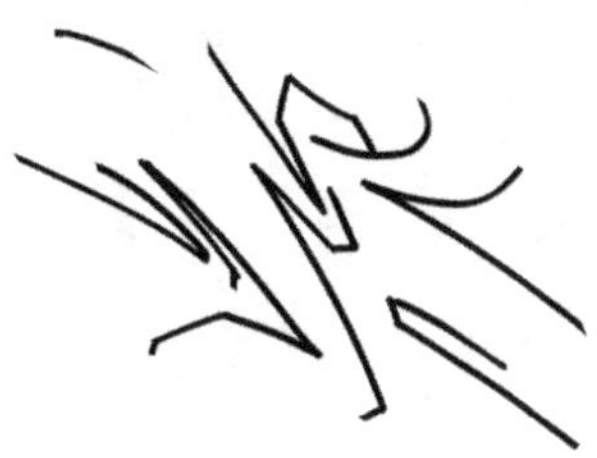

STEP 1
Finish outline

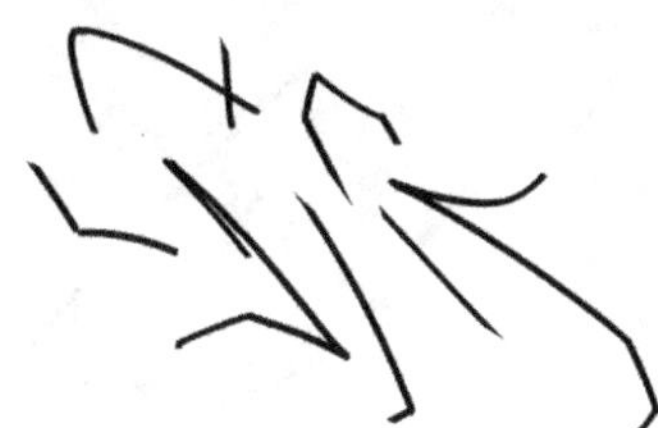

STEP 2
Finish outline

STEP 3
Do it yourself!

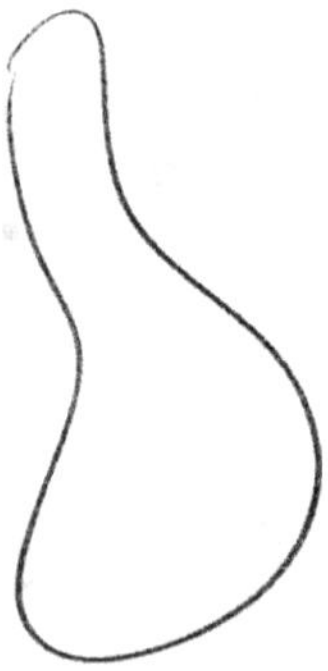

STEP 1
Basic shapes

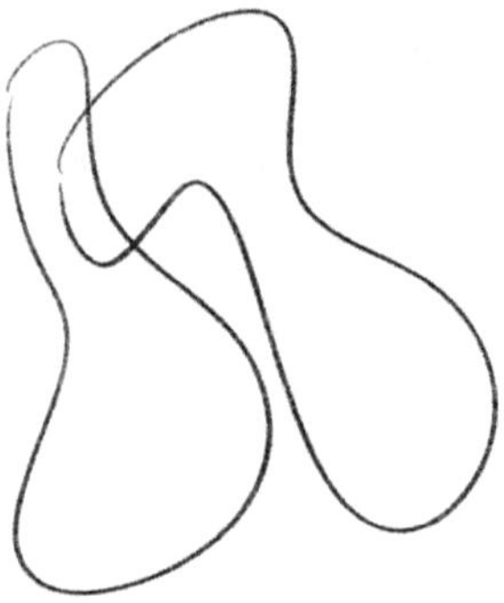

STEP 2
Last shapes and add-ons

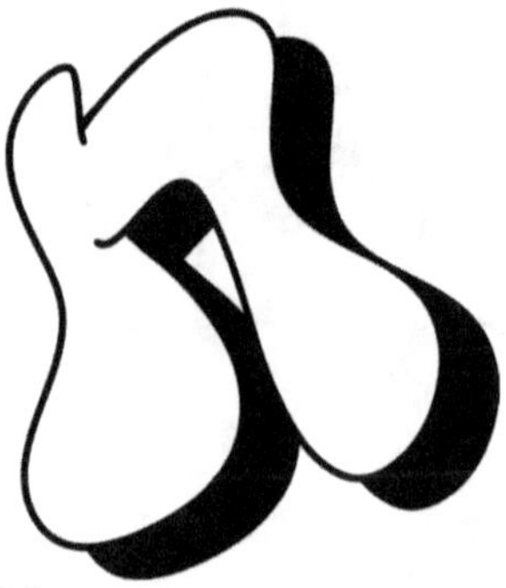

STEP 3
Outline and shadow

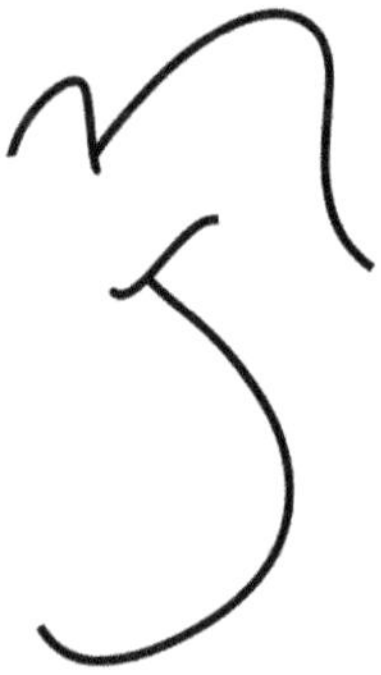

STEP 1
Finish outline

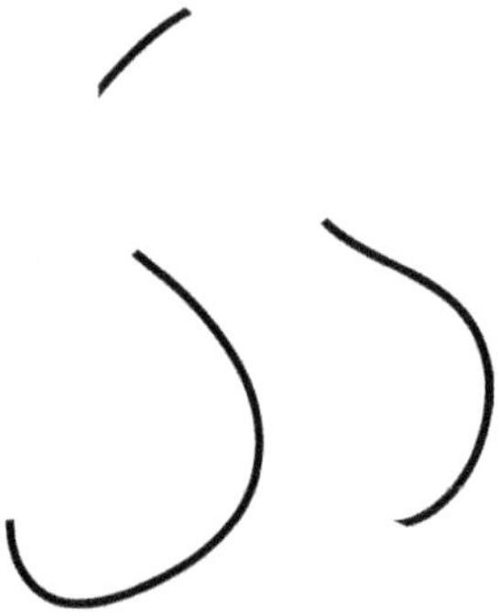

STEP 2
Finish outline and shadow

STEP 3
Do it yourself!

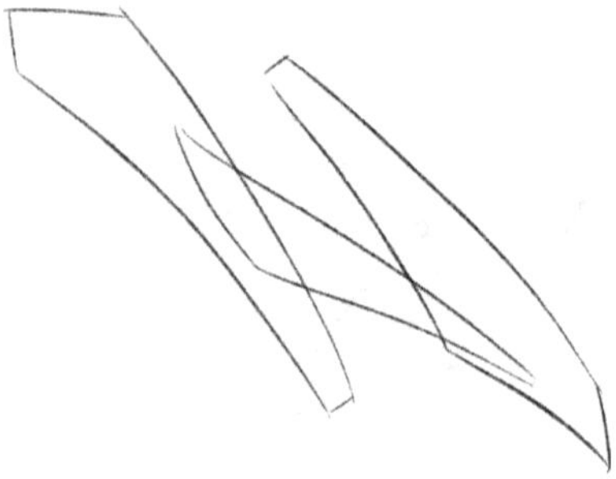

STEP 1
Basic shapes

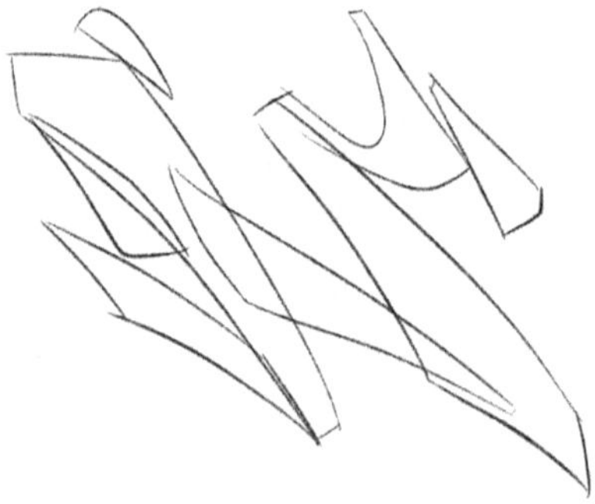

STEP 2
Last shapes and add-ons

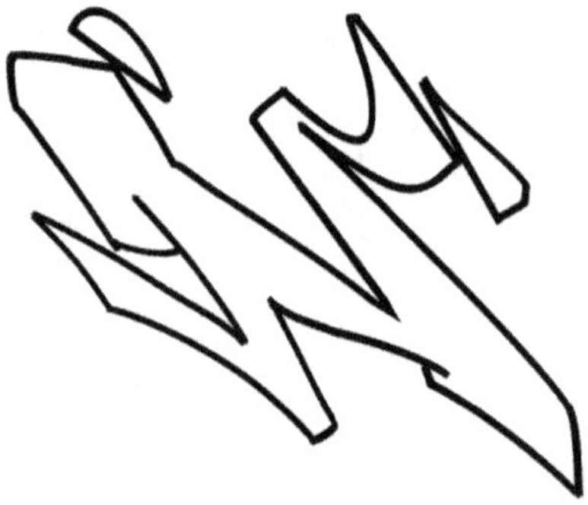

STEP 3
Outline

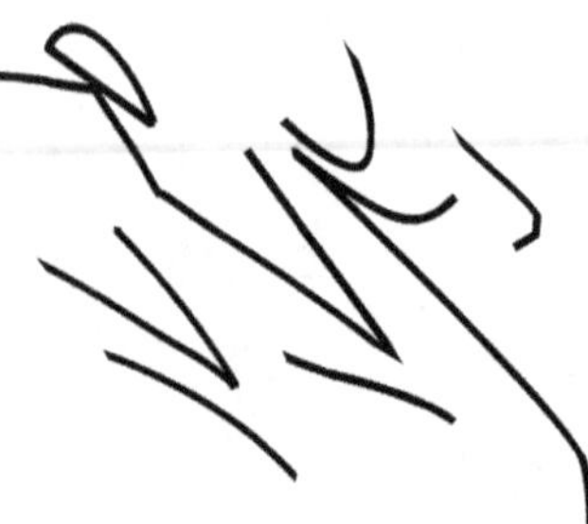

STEP 1
Finish outline

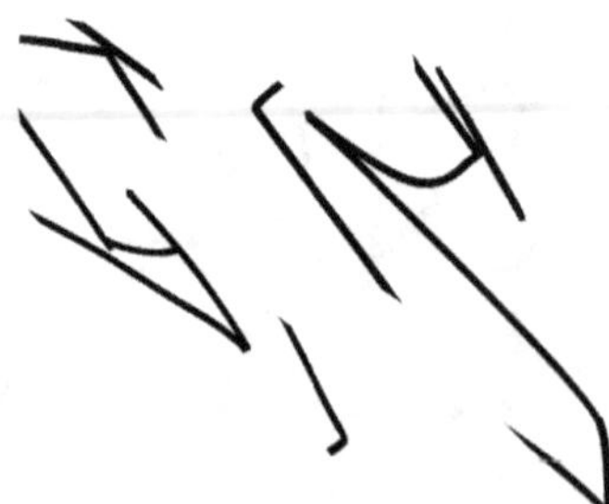

STEP 2
Finish outline

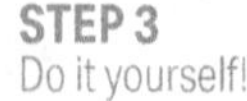

STEP 3
Do it yourself!

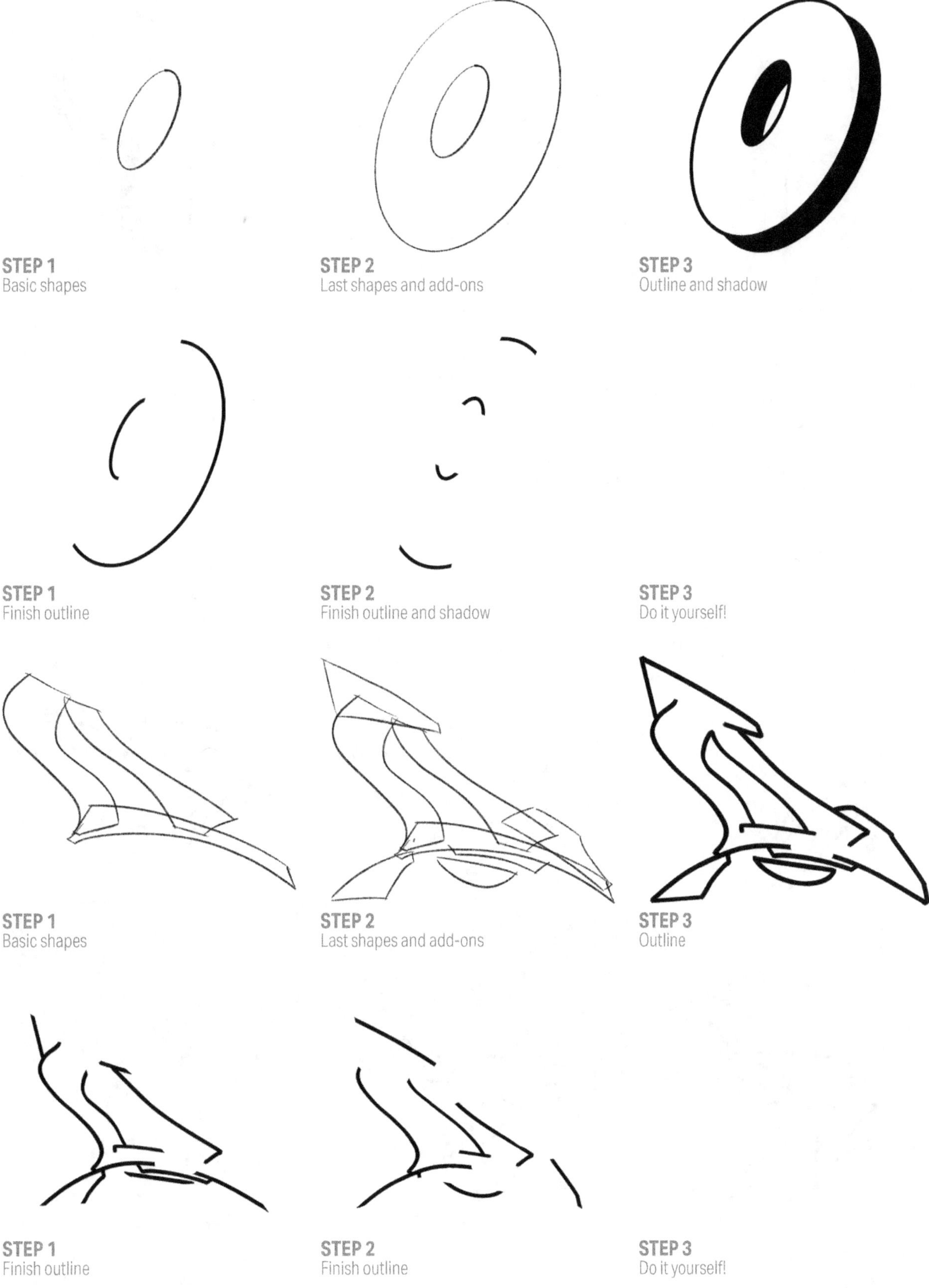

STEP 1
Basic shapes

STEP 2
Last shapes and add-ons

STEP 3
Outline and shadow

STEP 1
Finish outline

STEP 2
Finish outline and shadow

STEP 3
Do it yourself!

STEP 1
Basic shapes

STEP 2
Last shapes and add-ons

STEP 3
Outline

STEP 1
Finish outline

STEP 2
Finish outline

STEP 3
Do it yourself!

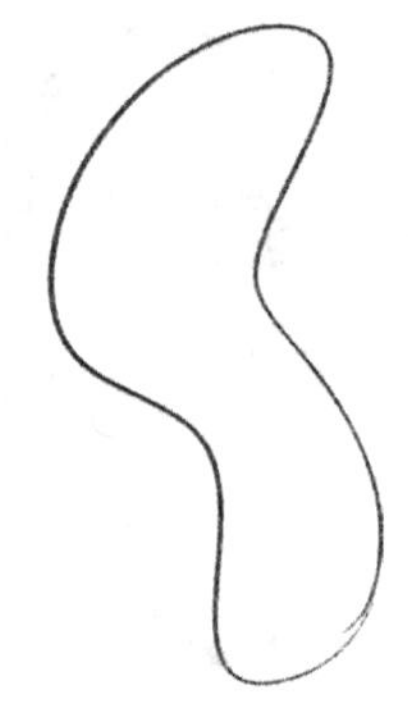

STEP 1
Basic shapes

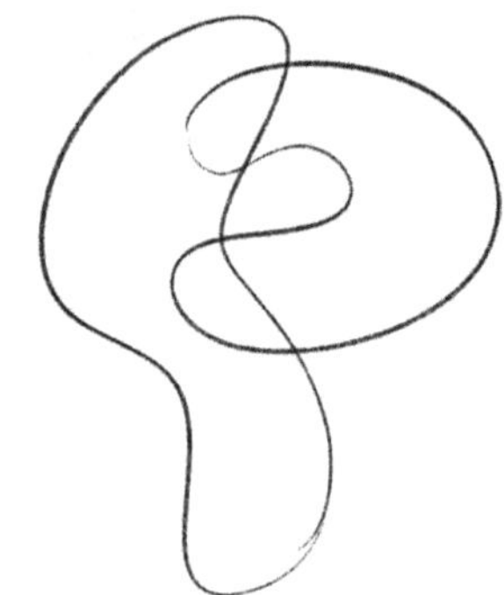

STEP 2
Last shapes and add-ons

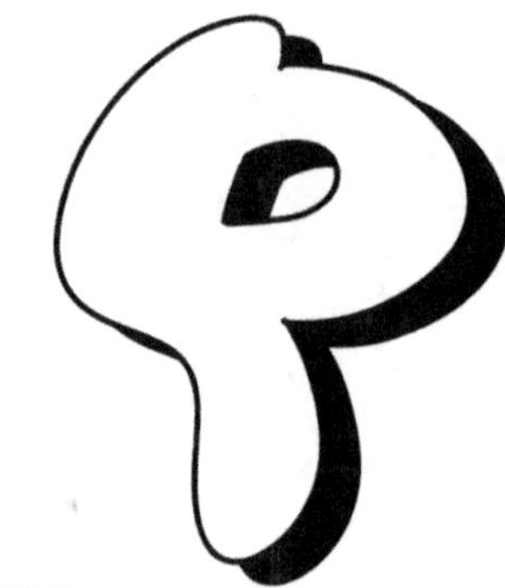

STEP 3
Outline and shadow

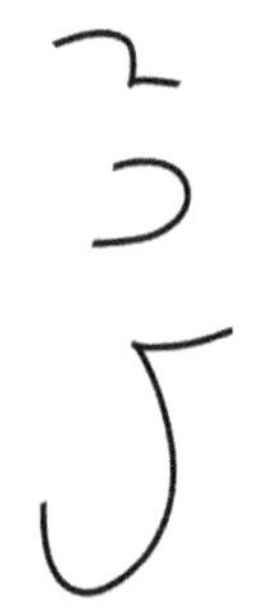

STEP 1
Finish outline

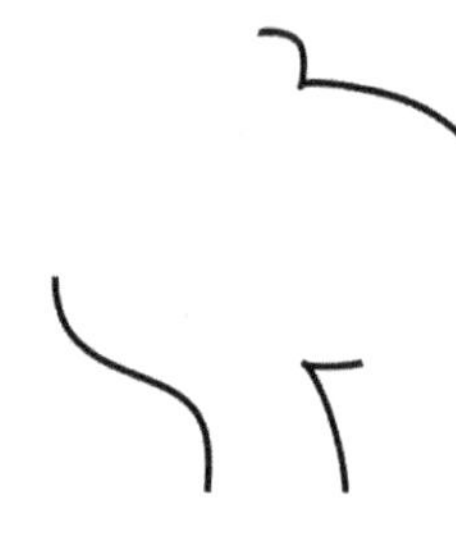
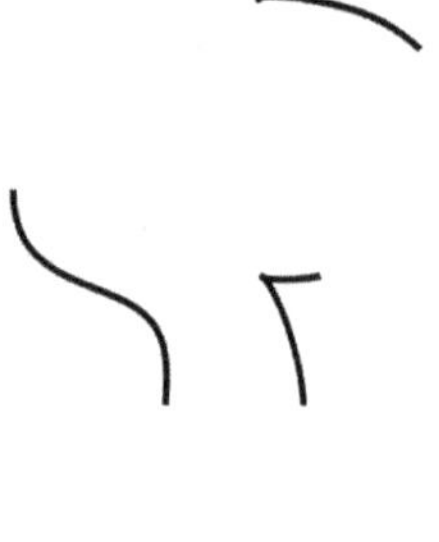

STEP 2
Finish outline and shadow

STEP 3
Do it yourself!

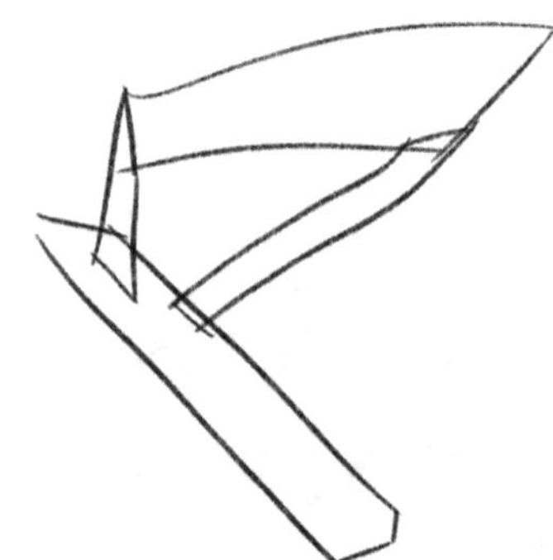

STEP 1
Basic shapes

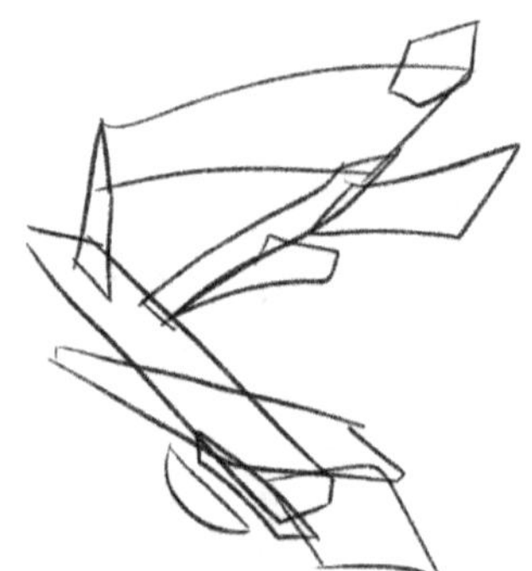

STEP 2
Last shapes and add-ons

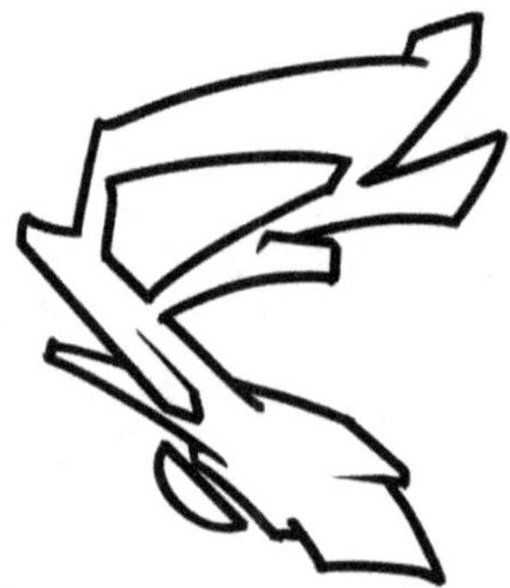

STEP 3
Outline

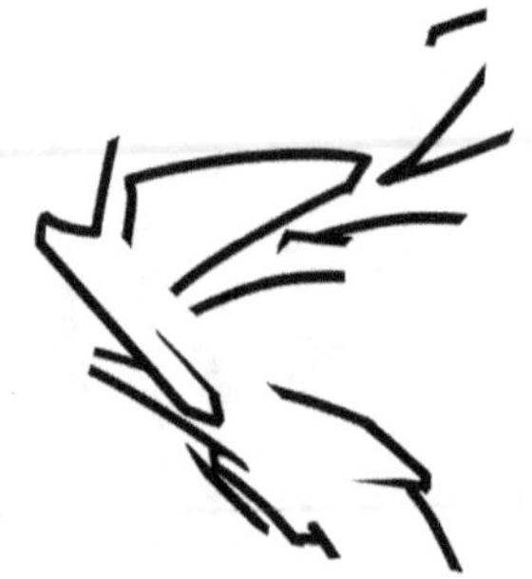

STEP 1
Finish outline

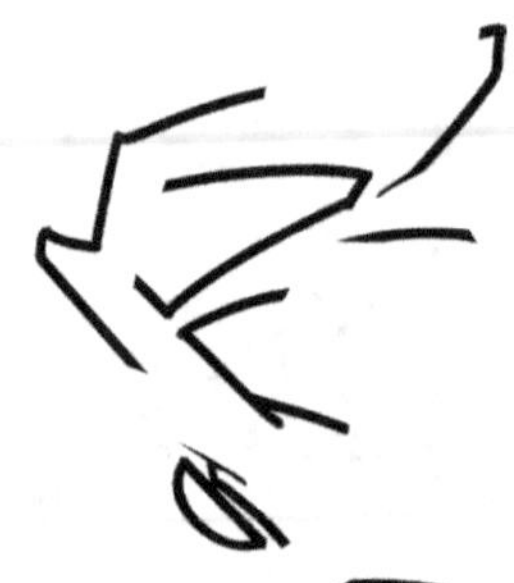

STEP 2
Finish outline

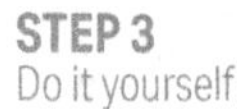

STEP 3
Do it yourself!

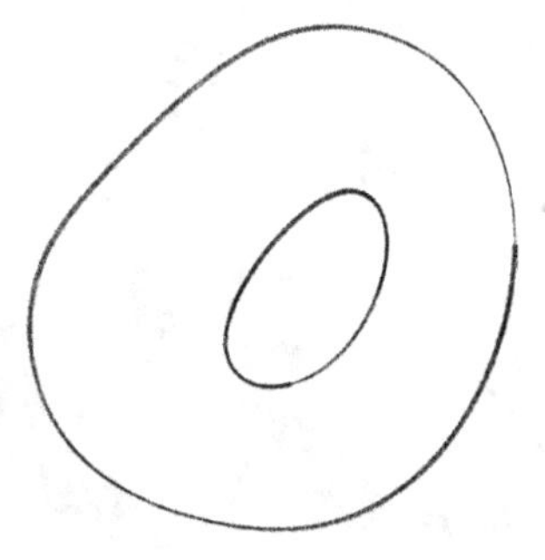

STEP 1
Basic shapes

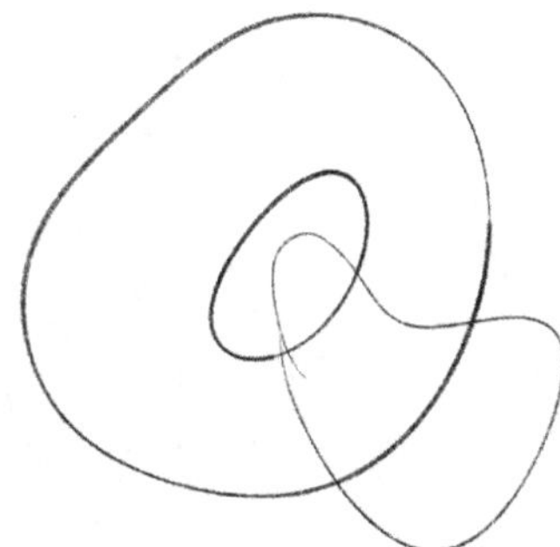

STEP 2
Last shapes and add-ons

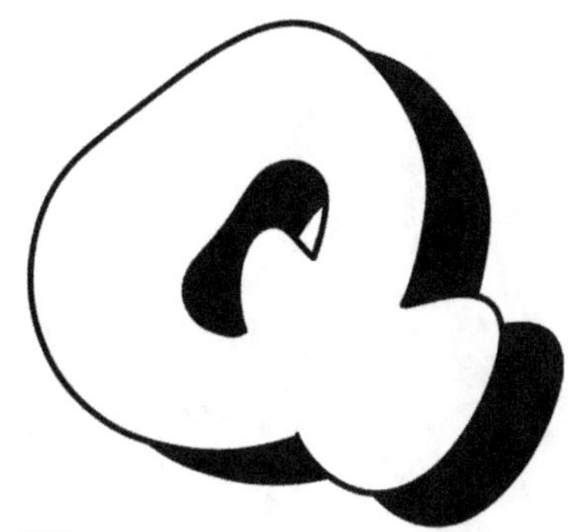

STEP 3
Outline and shadow

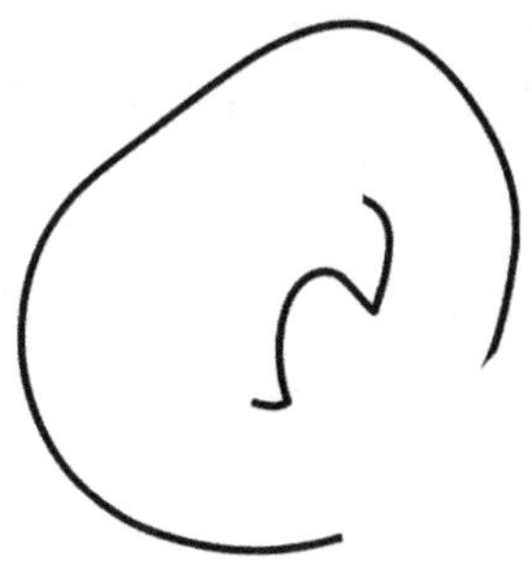

STEP 1
Finish outline

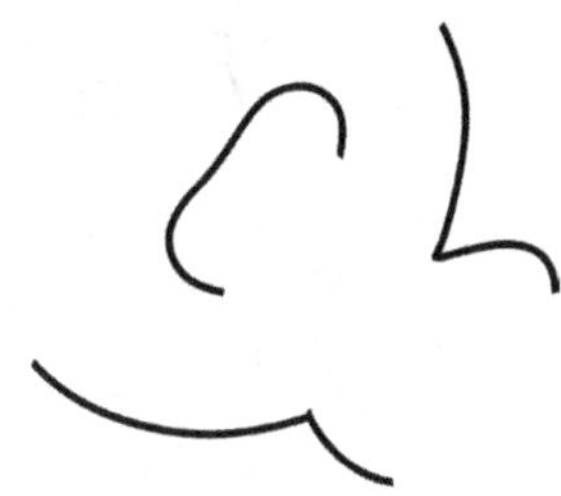

STEP 2
Finish outline and shadow

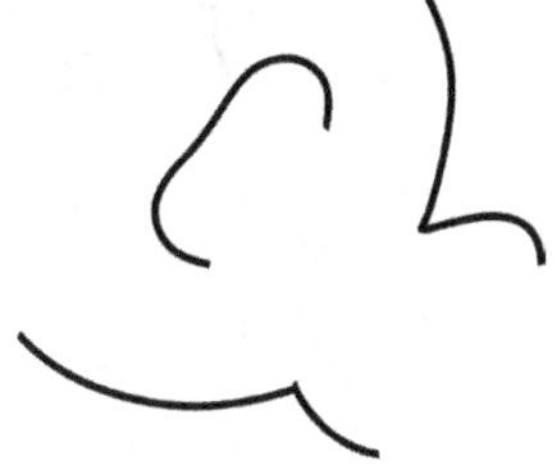

STEP 3
Do it yourself!

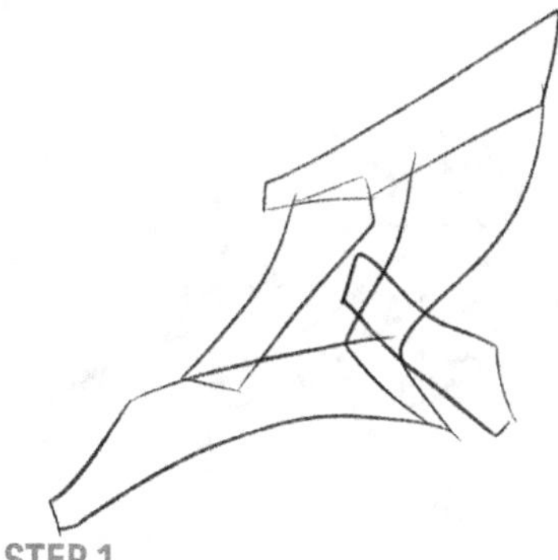

STEP 1
Basic shapes

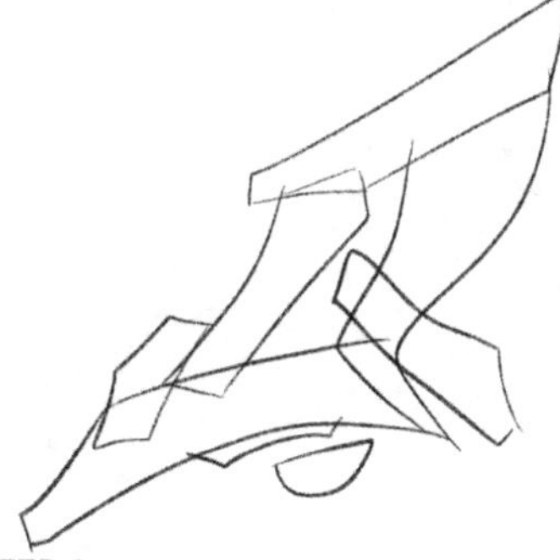

STEP 2
Last shapes and add-ons

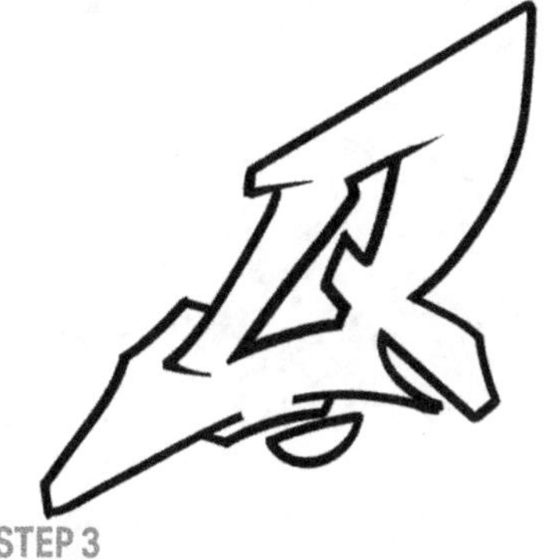

STEP 3
Outline

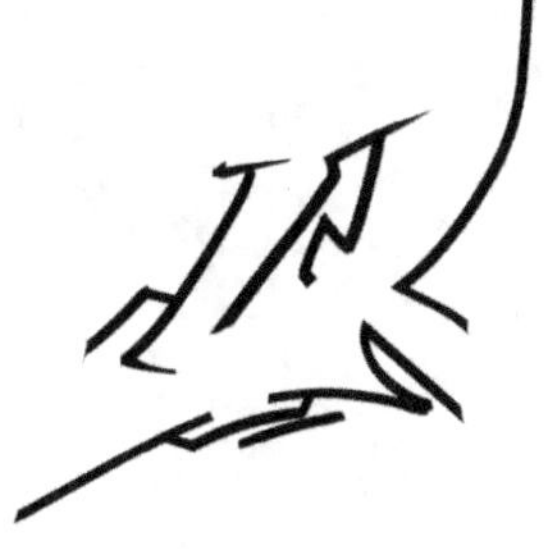

STEP 1
Finish outline

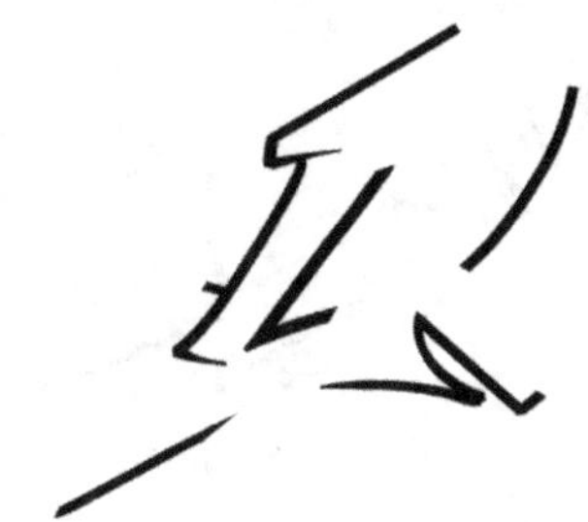

STEP 2
Finish outline

STEP 3
Do it yourself!

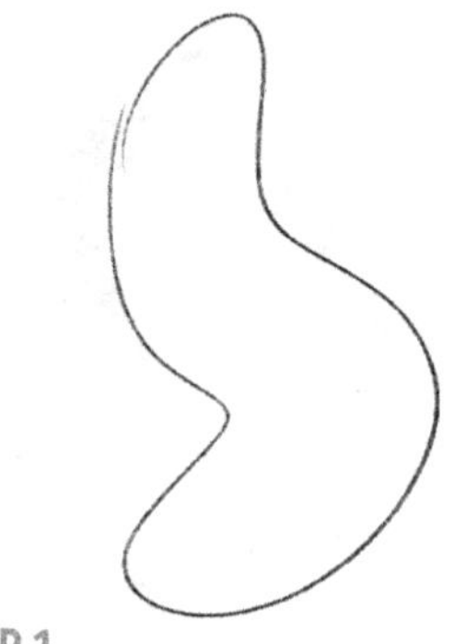
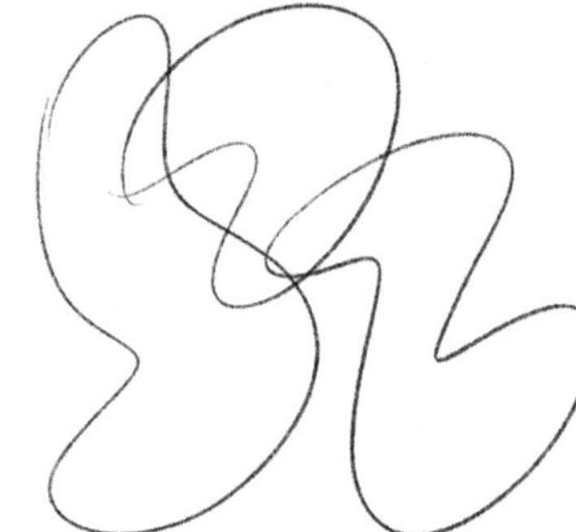
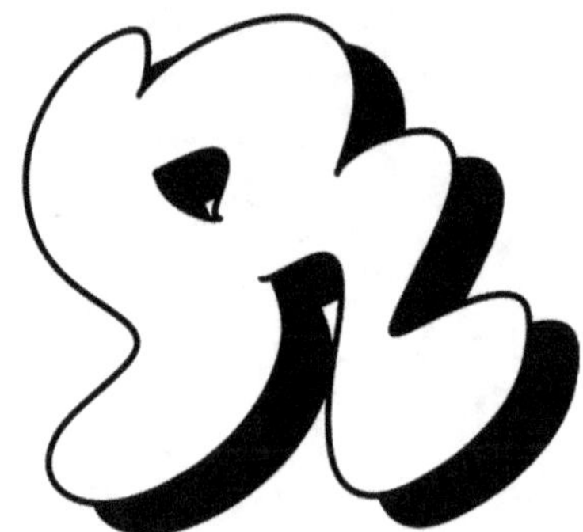

STEP 1
Basic shapes

STEP 2
Last shapes and add-ons

STEP 3
Outline and shadow

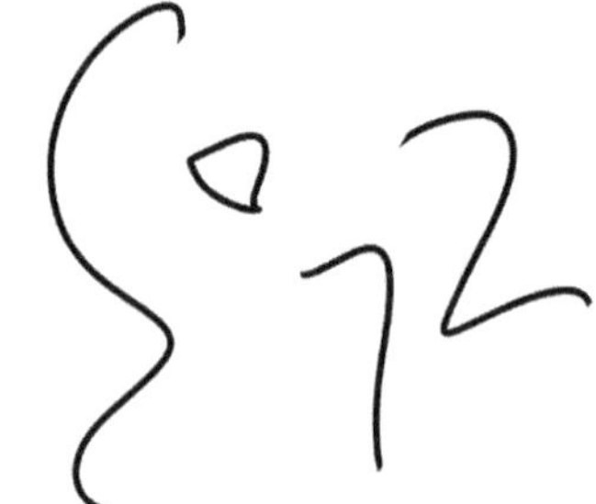
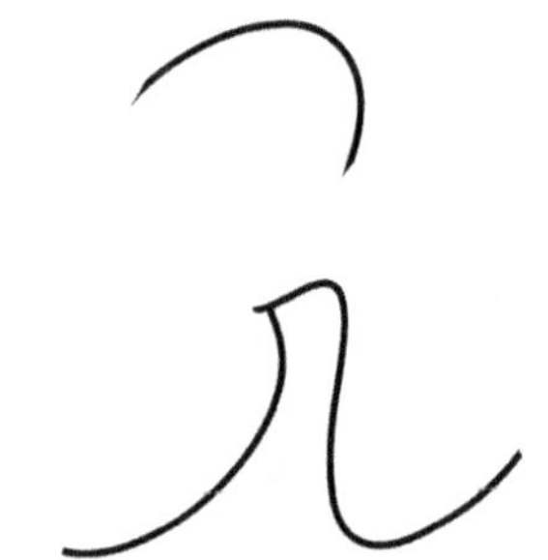
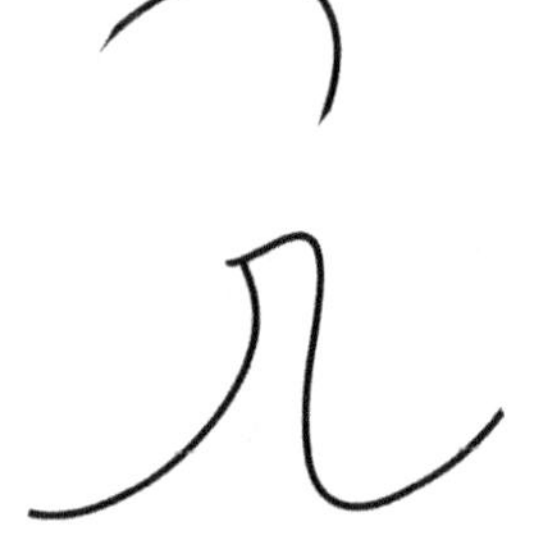

STEP 1
Finish outline

STEP 2
Finish outline and shadow

STEP 3
Do it yourself!

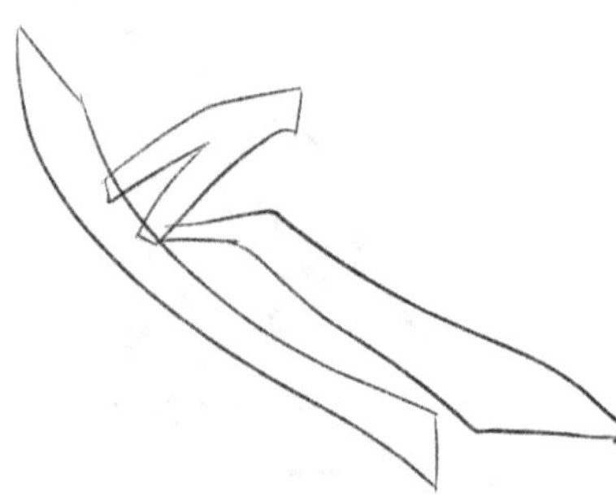
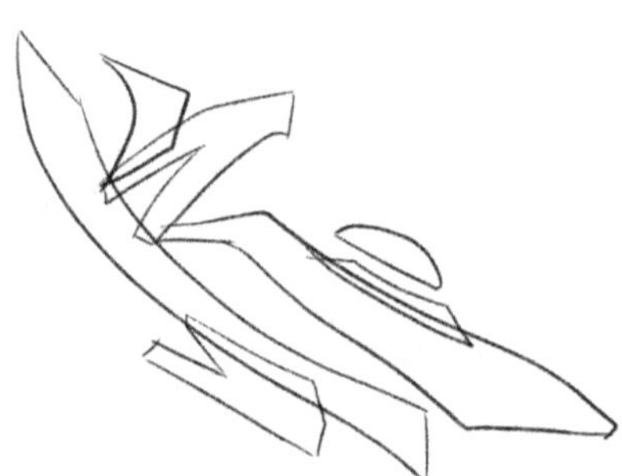
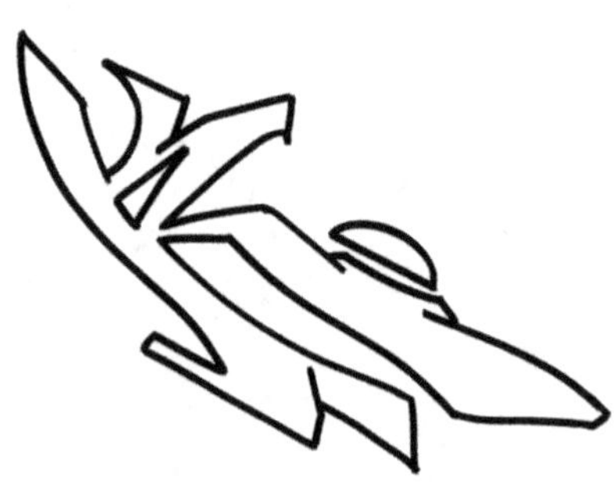

STEP 1
Basic shapes

STEP 2
Last shapes and add-ons

STEP 3
Outline

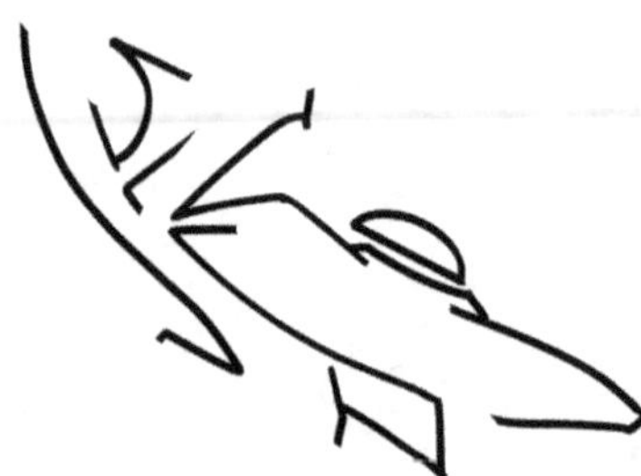
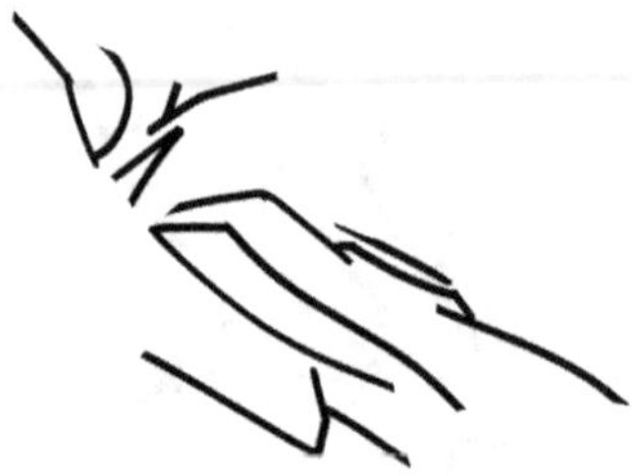

STEP 1
Finish outline

STEP 2
Finish outline

STEP 3
Do it yourself!

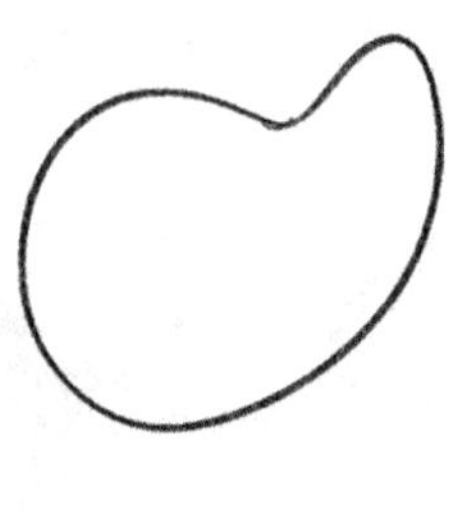
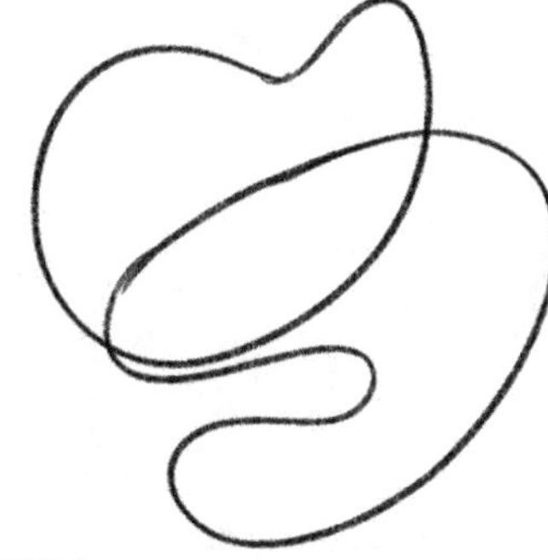
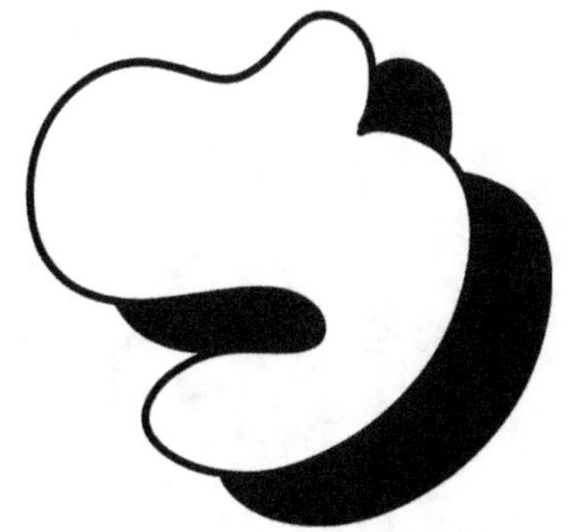

STEP 1
Basic shapes

STEP 2
Last shapes and add-ons

STEP 3
Outline and shadow

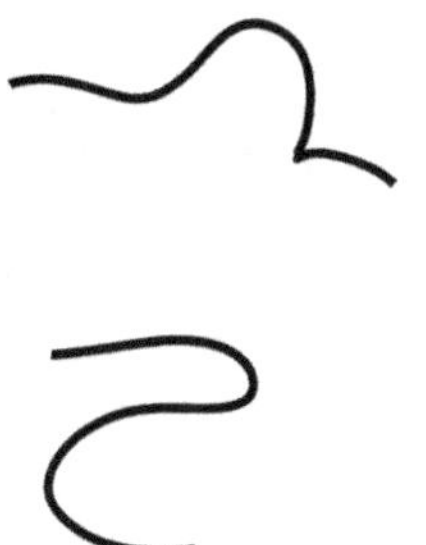
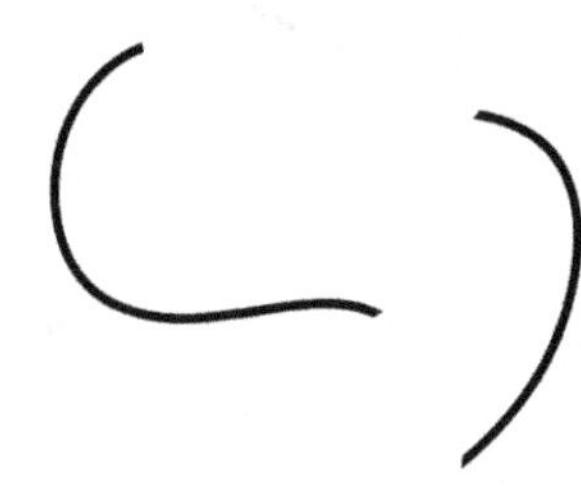
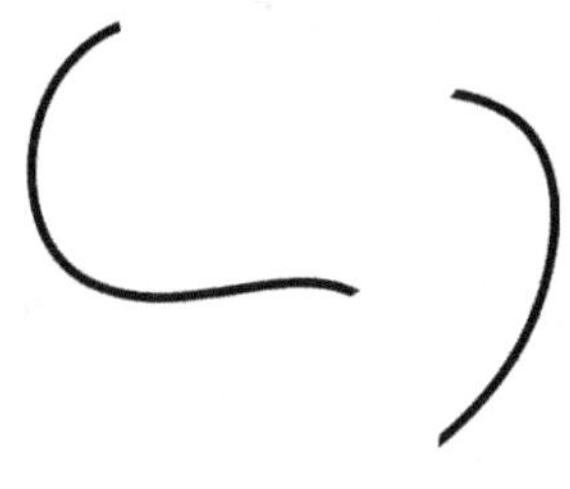

STEP 1
Finish outline

STEP 2
Finish outline and shadow

STEP 3
Do it yourself!

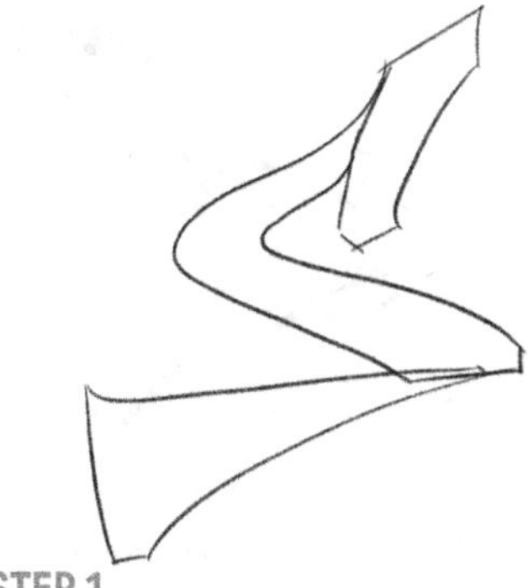
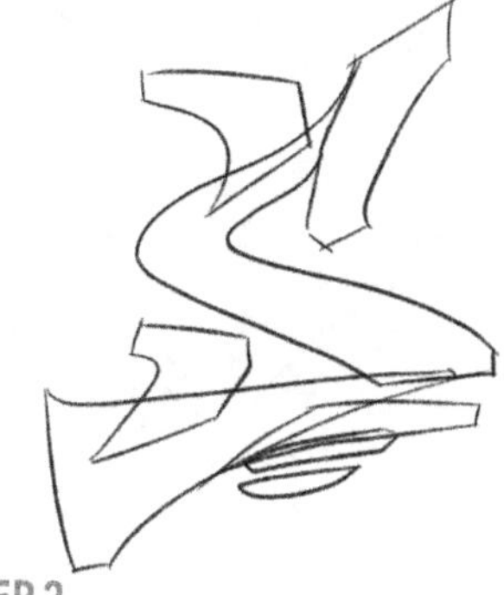
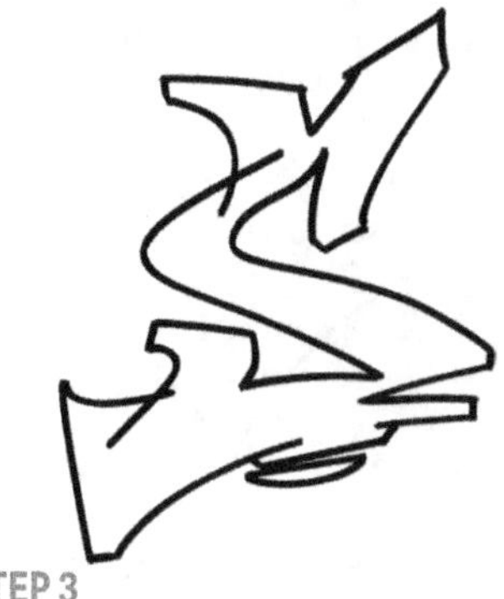

STEP 1
Basic shapes

STEP 2
Last shapes and add-ons

STEP 3
Outline

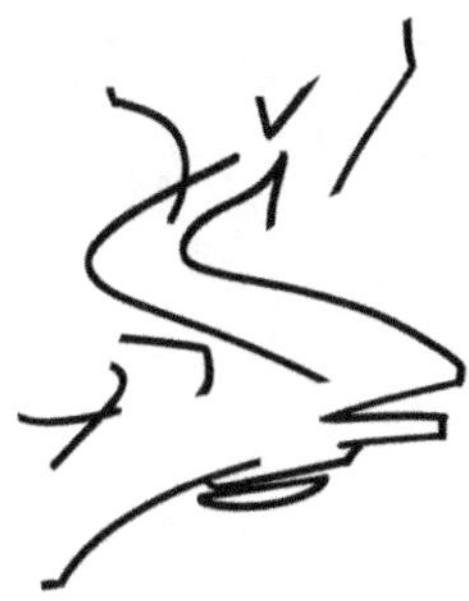
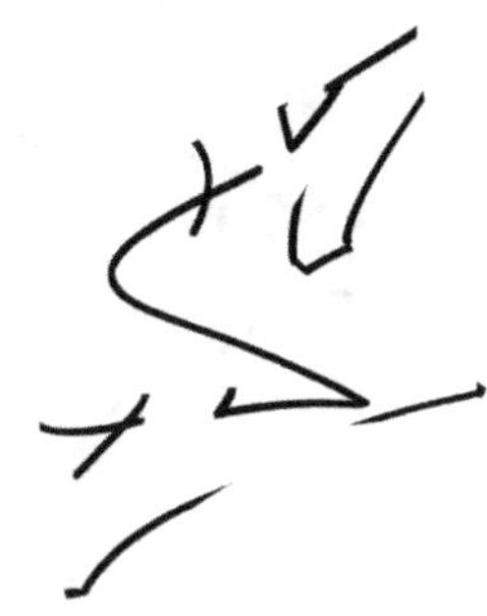

STEP 1
Finish outline

STEP 2
Finish outline

STEP 3
Do it yourself!

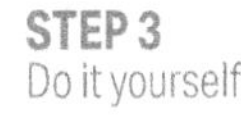

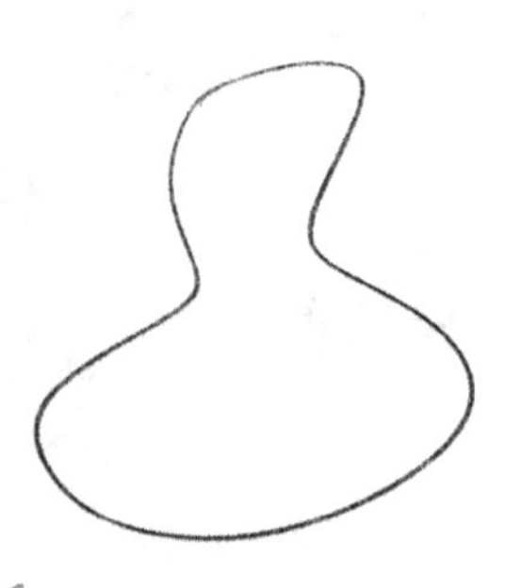

STEP 1
Basic shapes

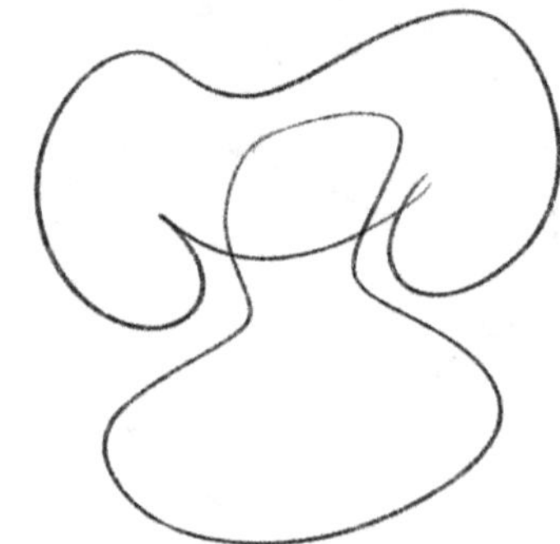

STEP 2
Last shapes and add-ons

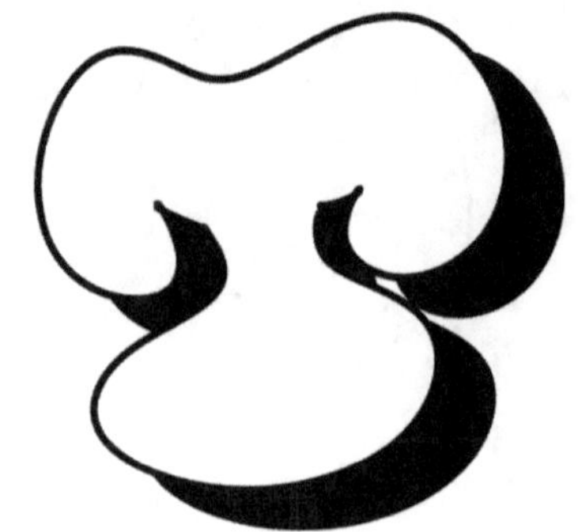

STEP 3
Outline and shadow

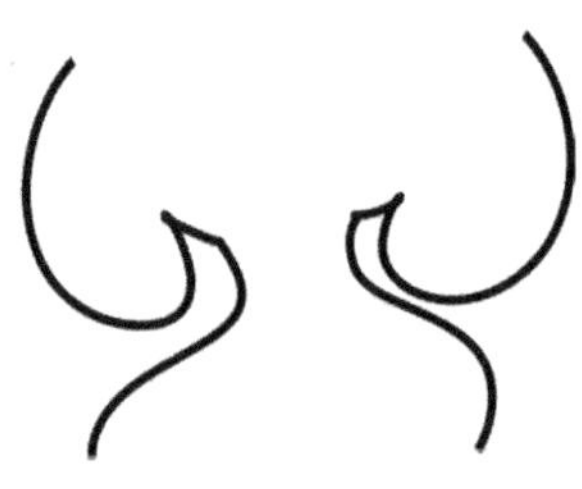

STEP 1
Finish outline

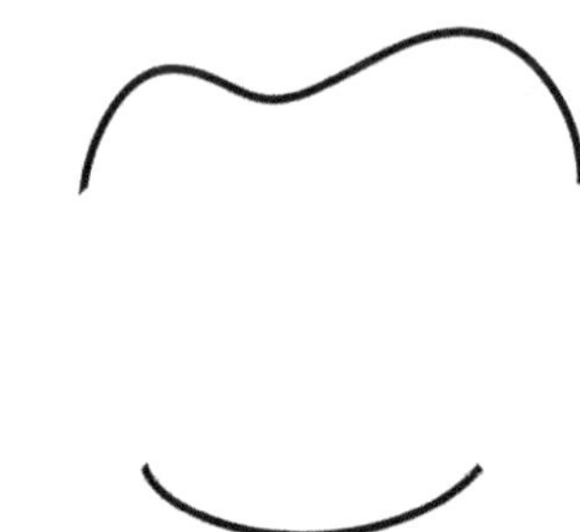
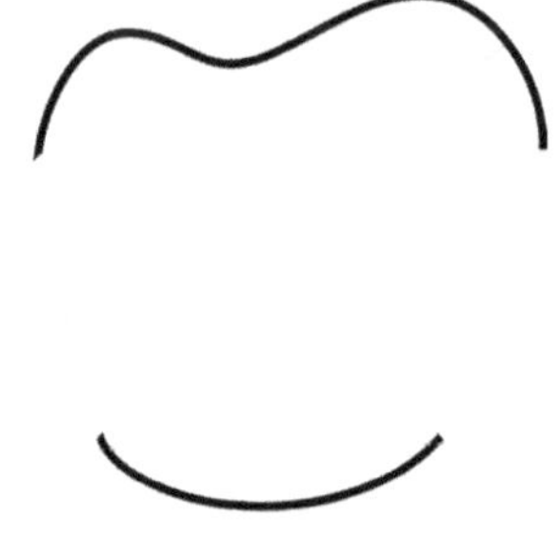

STEP 2
Finish outline and shadow

STEP 3
Do it yourself!

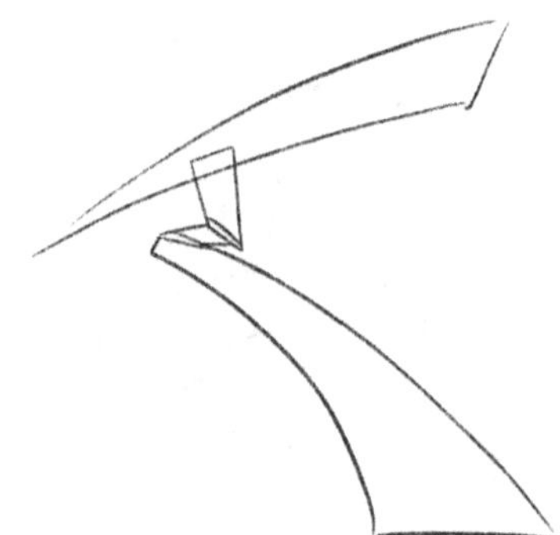

STEP 1
Basic shapes

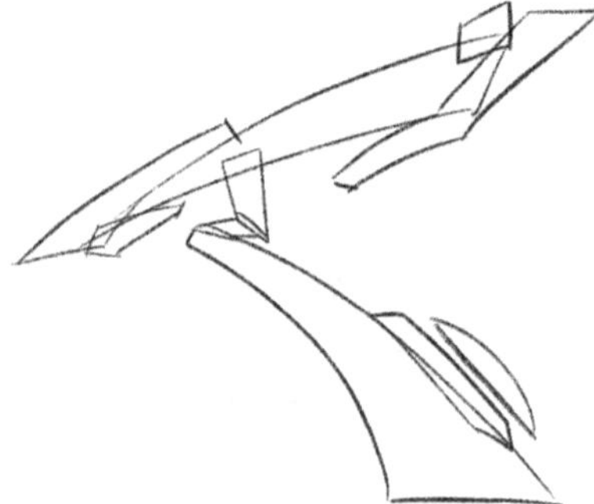

STEP 2
Last shapes and add-ons

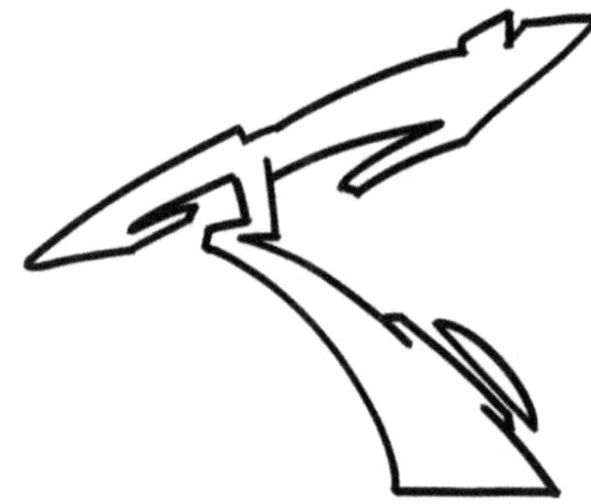

STEP 3
Outline

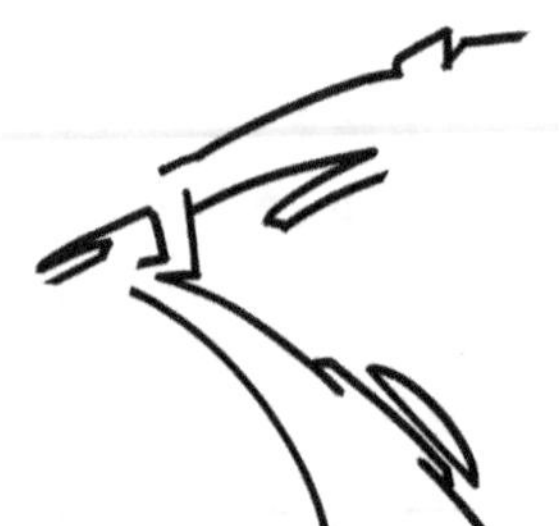

STEP 1
Finish outline

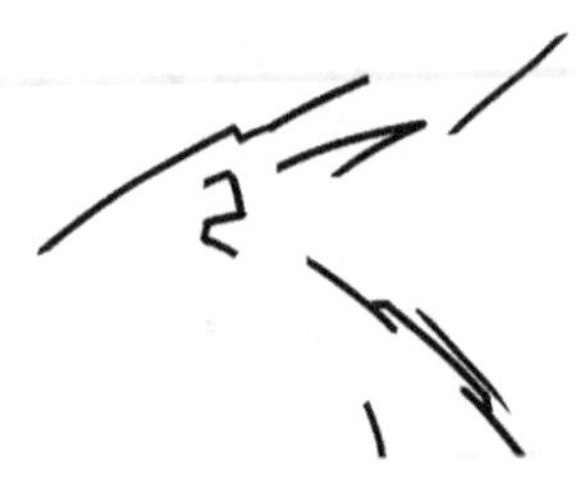

STEP 2
Finish outline

STEP 3
Do it yourself!

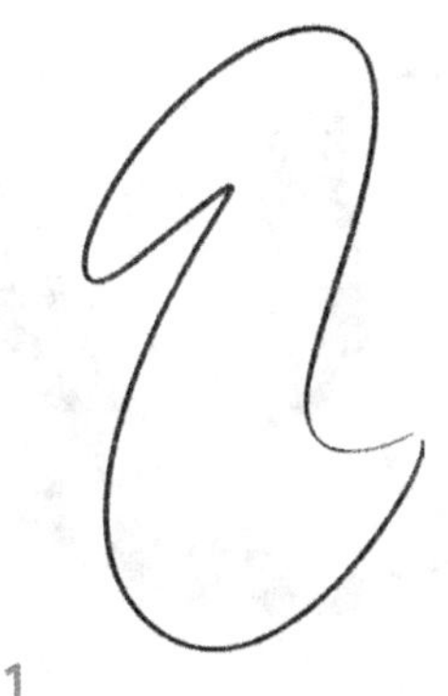

STEP 1
Basic shapes

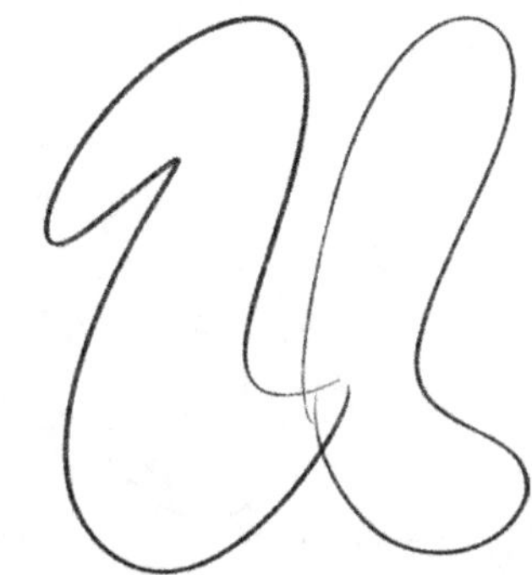

STEP 2
Last shapes and add-ons

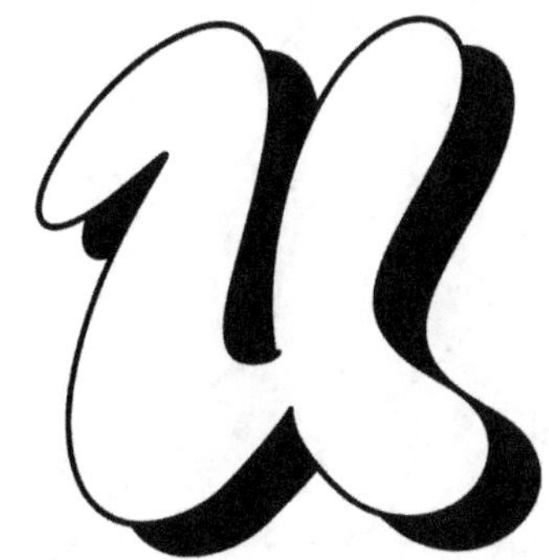

STEP 3
Outline and shadow

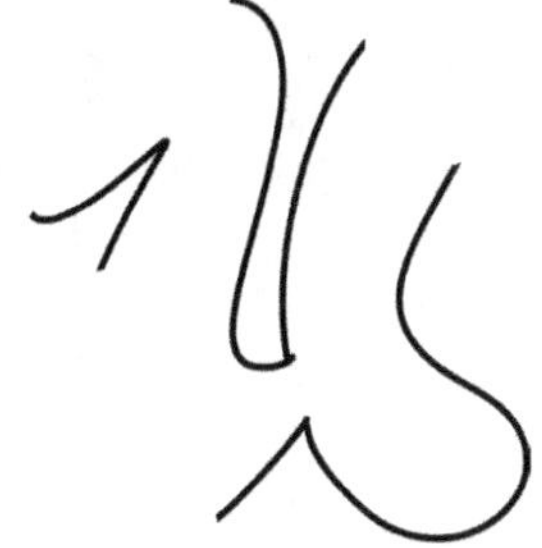

STEP 1
Finish outline

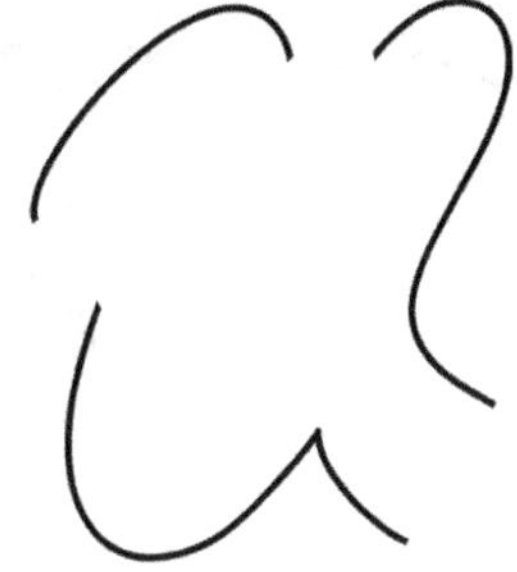

STEP 2
Finish outline and shadow

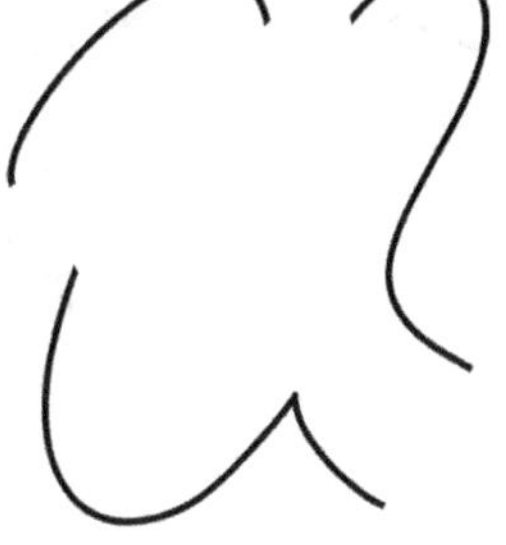

STEP 3
Do it yourself!

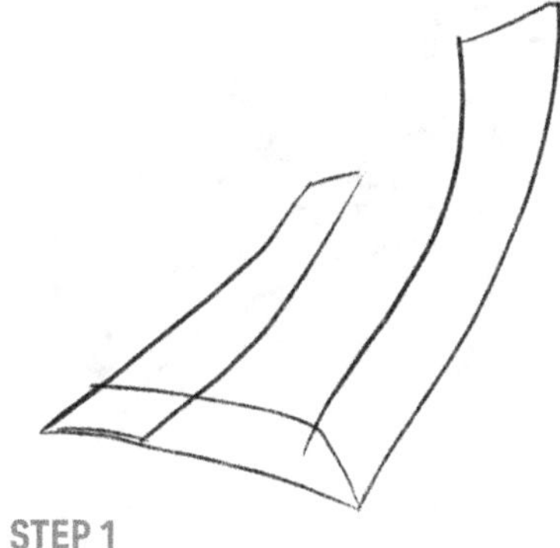

STEP 1
Basic shapes

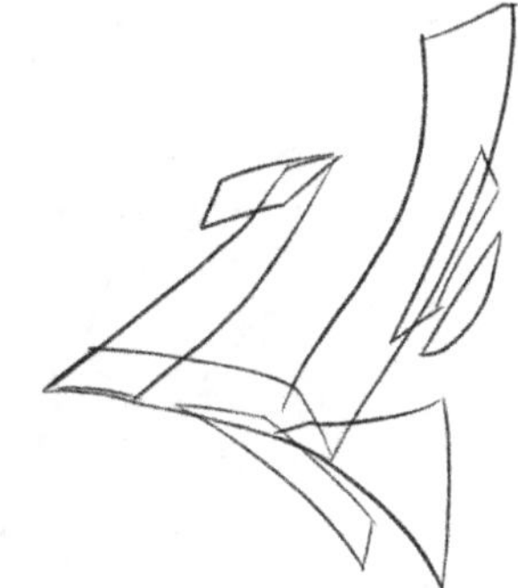

STEP 2
Last shapes and add-ons

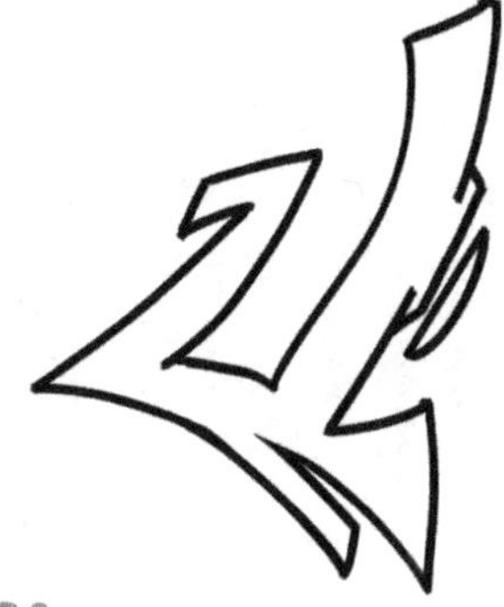

STEP 3
Outline

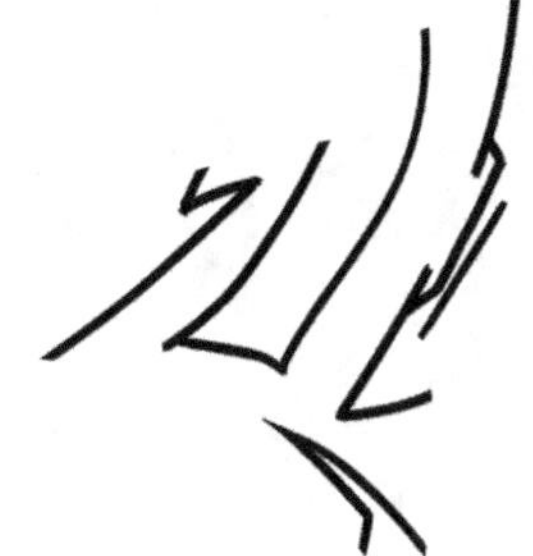

STEP 1
Finish outline

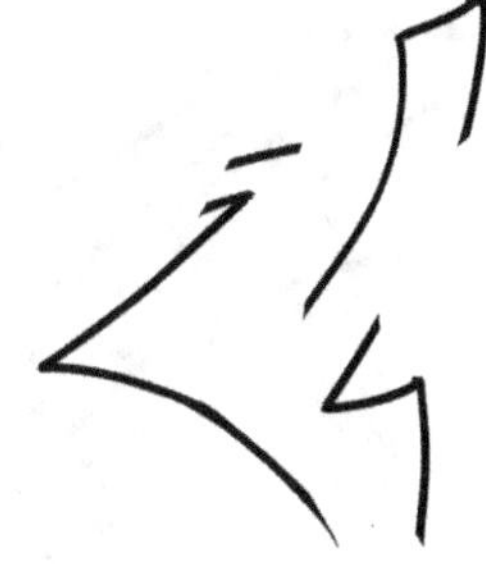

STEP 2
Finish outline

STEP 3
Do it yourself!

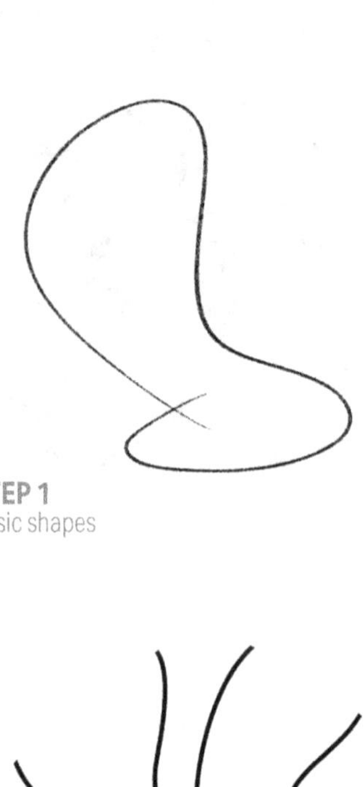
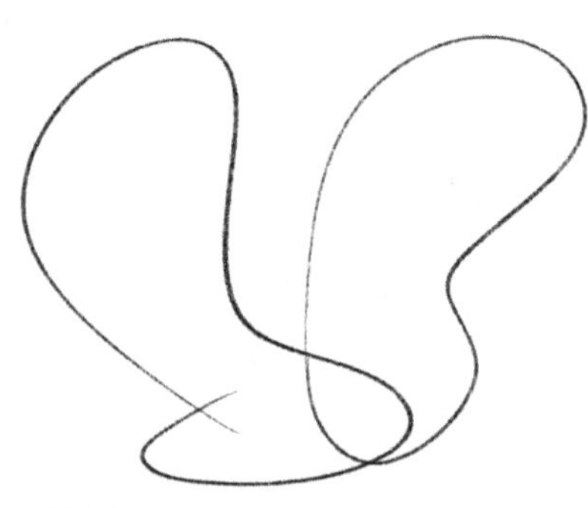
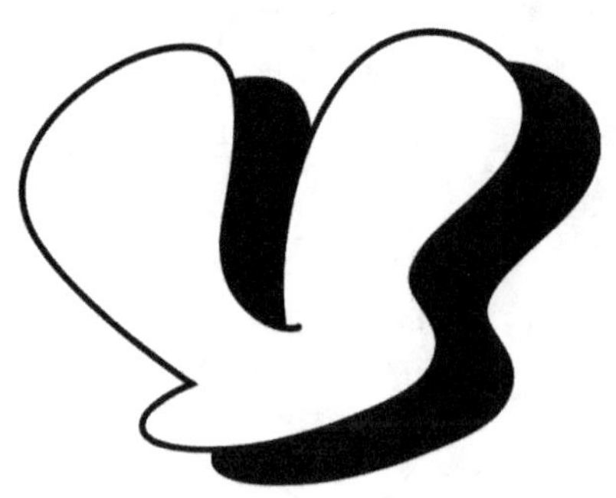

STEP 1
Basic shapes

STEP 2
Last shapes and add-ons

STEP 3
Outline and shadow

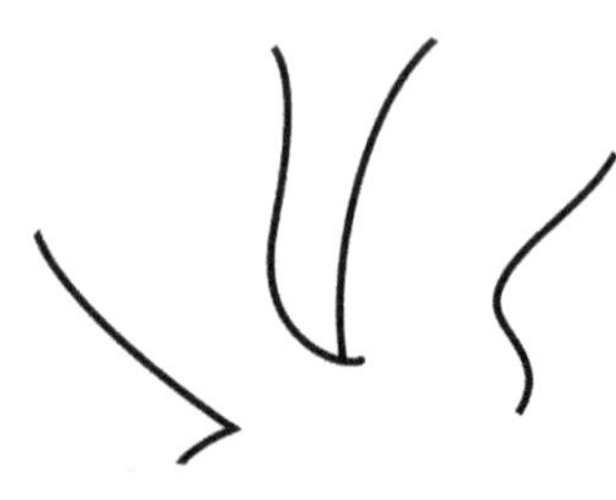
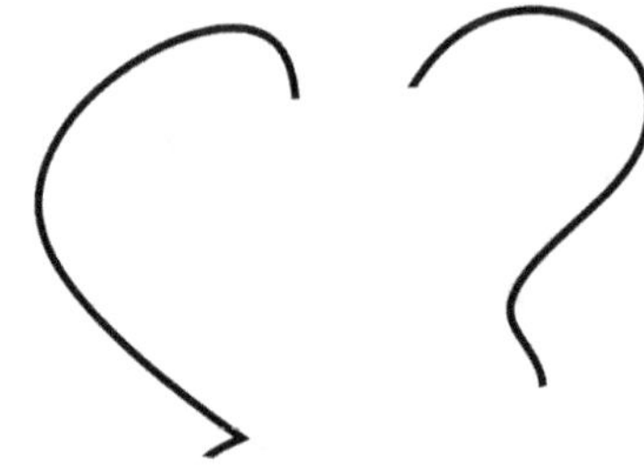

STEP 1
Finish outline

STEP 2
Finish outline and shadow

STEP 3
Do it yourself!

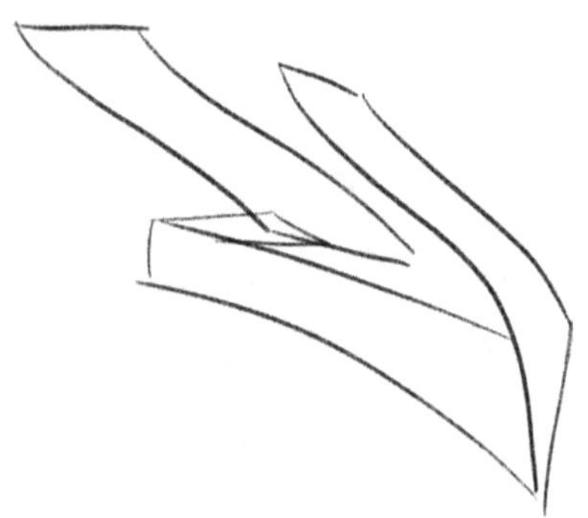
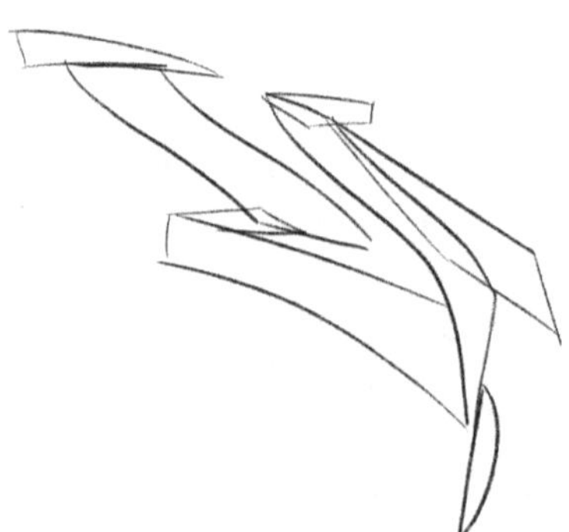
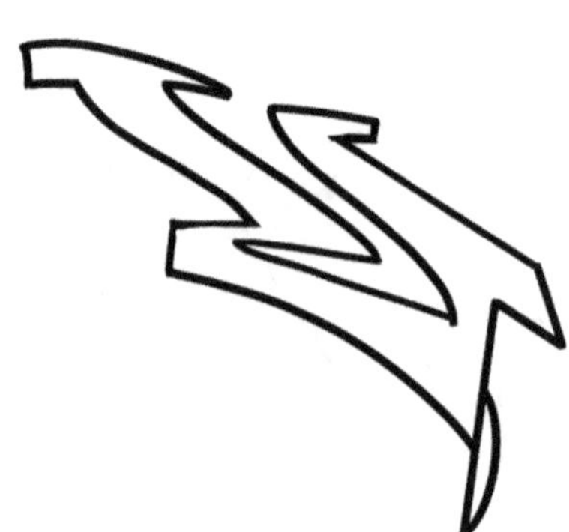

STEP 1
Basic shapes

STEP 2
Last shapes and add-ons

STEP 3
Outline

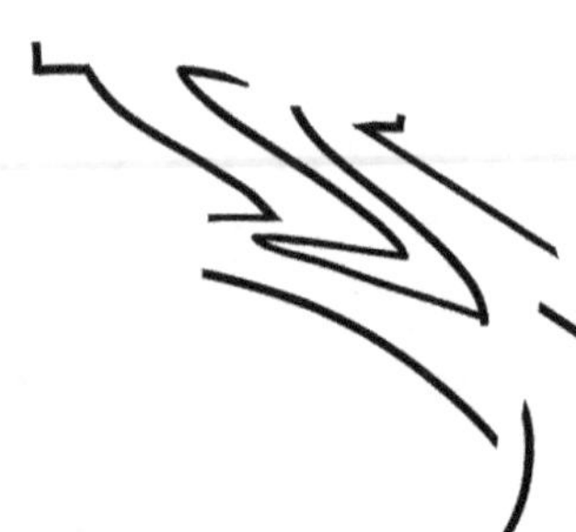
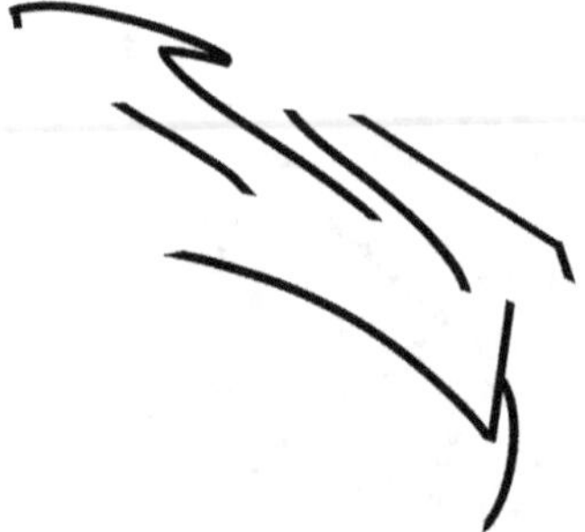

STEP 1
Finish outline

STEP 2
Finish outline

STEP 3
Do it yourself!

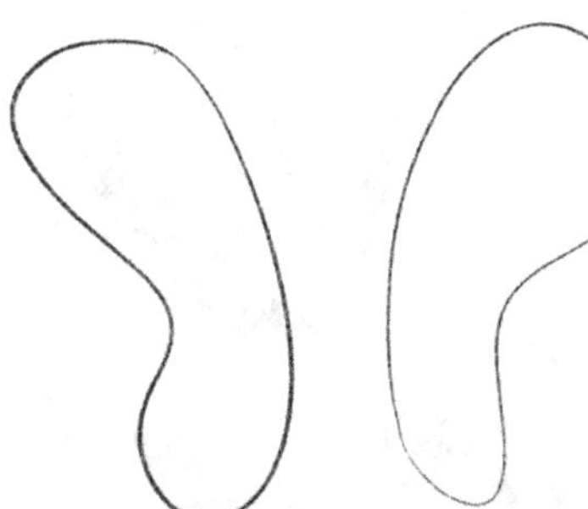

STEP 1
Basic shapes

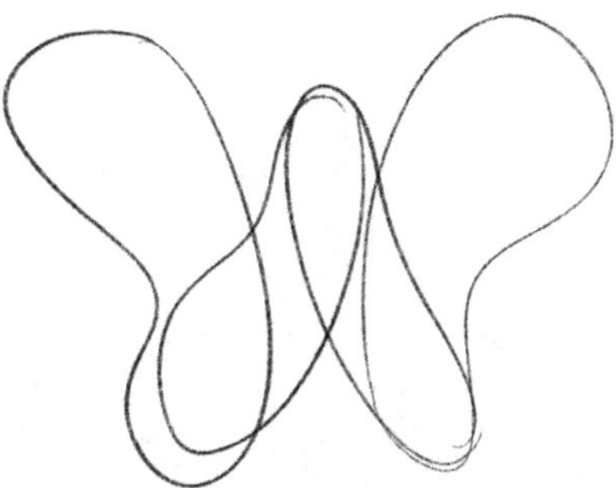

STEP 2
Last shapes and add-ons

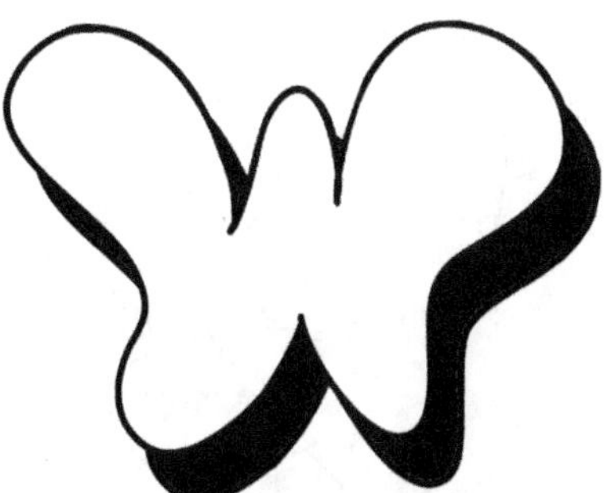

STEP 3
Outline and shadow

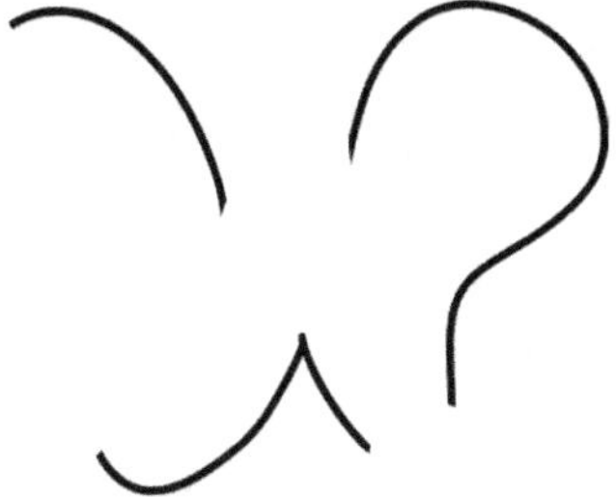

STEP 1
Finish outline

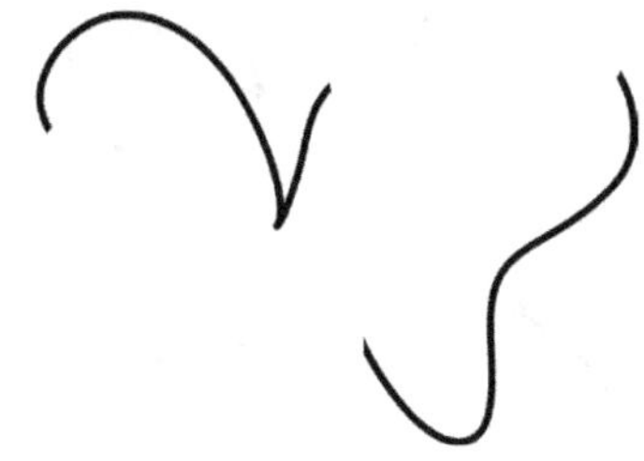

STEP 2
Finish outline and shadow

STEP 3
Do it yourself!

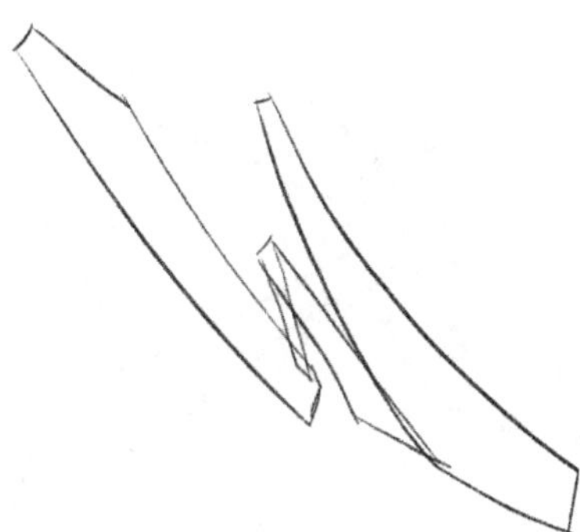

STEP 1
Basic shapes

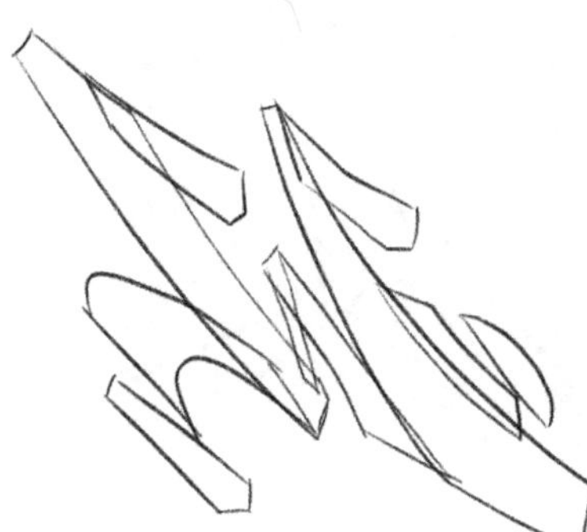

STEP 2
Last shapes and add-ons

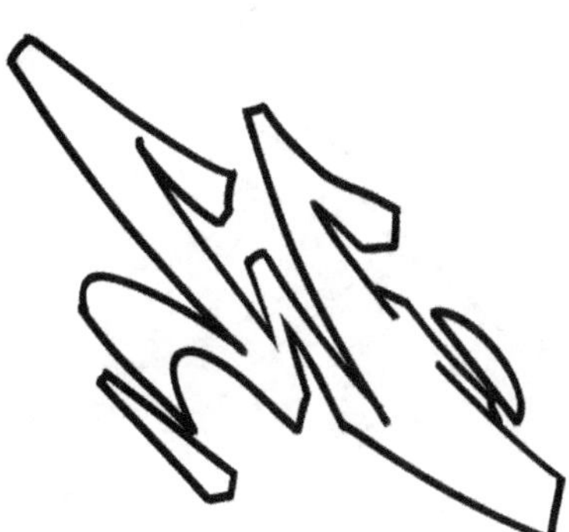

STEP 3
Outline

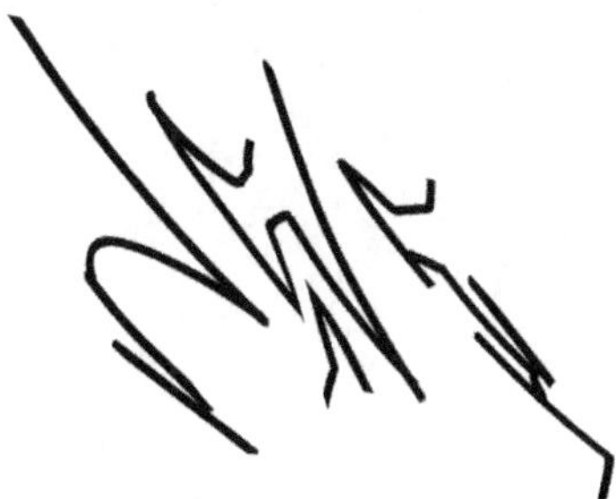

STEP 1
Finish outline

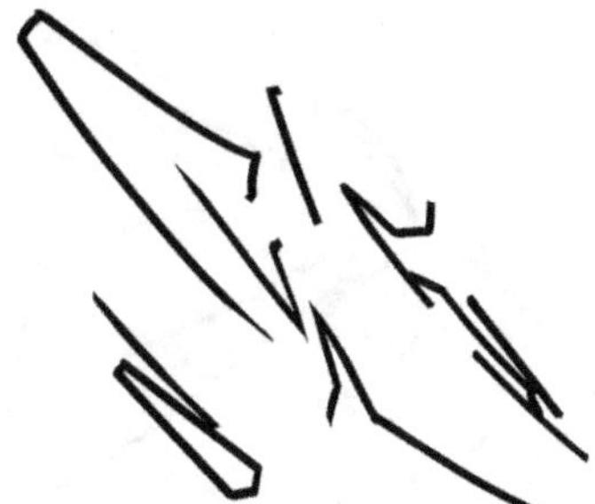

STEP 2
Finish outline

STEP 3
Do it yourself!

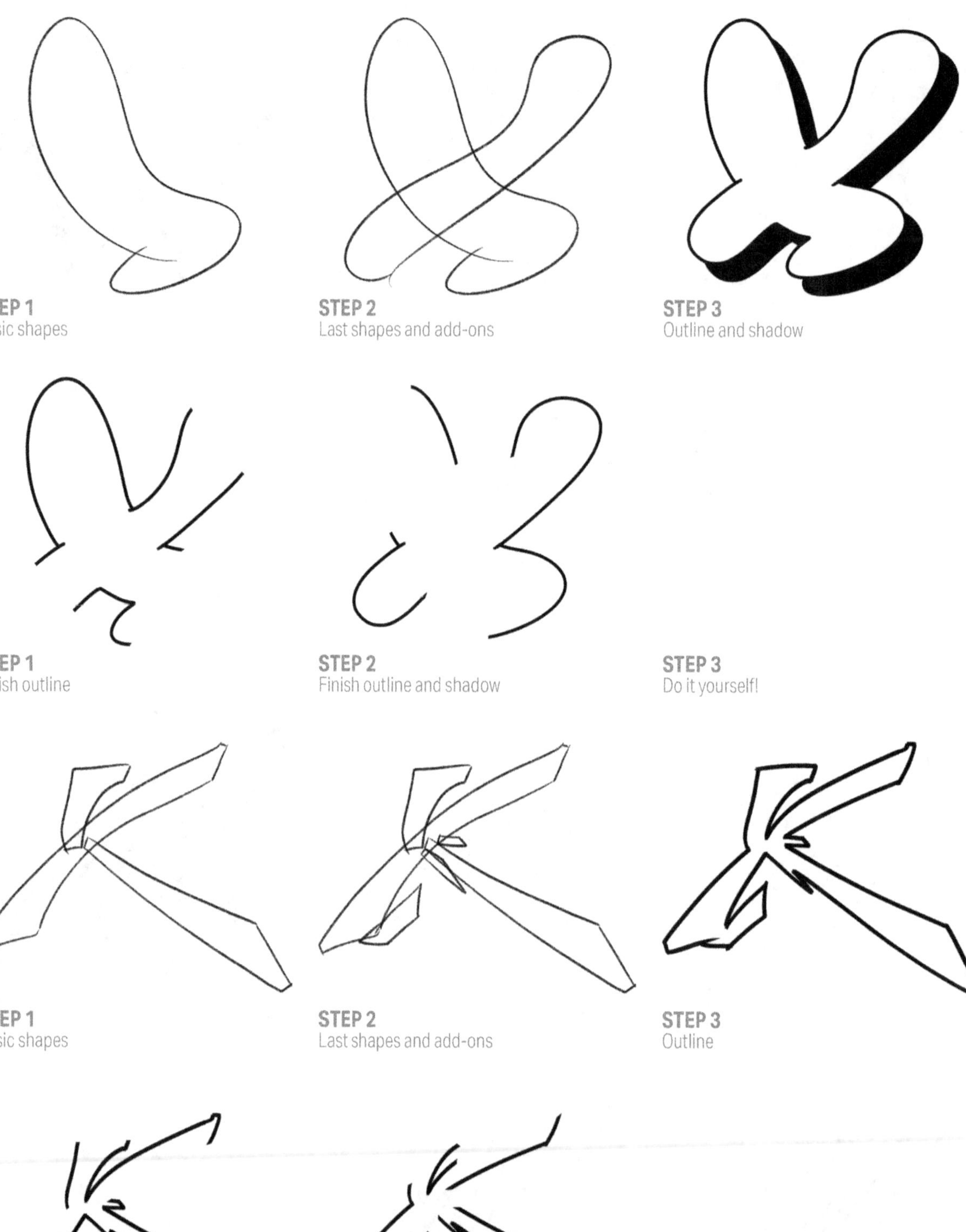

STEP 1
Basic shapes
STEP 2
Last shapes and add-ons
STEP 3
Outline and shadow
STEP 1
Finish outline
STEP 2
Finish outline and shadow
STEP 3
Do it yourself!
STEP 1
Basic shapes
STEP 2
Last shapes and add-ons
STEP 3
Outline
STEP 1
Finish outline
STEP 2
Finish outline
STEP 3
Do it yourself!

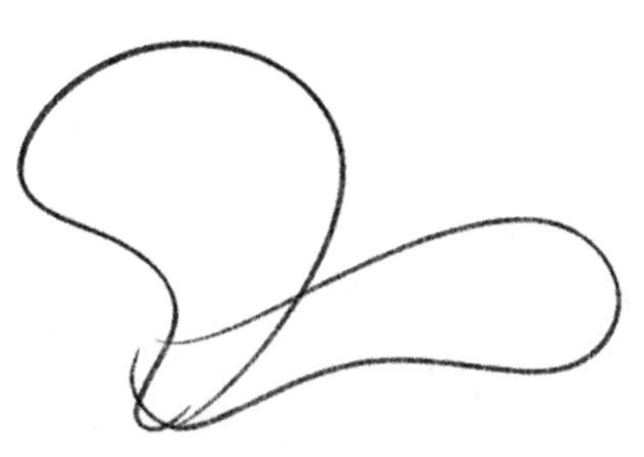

STEP 1
Basic shapes

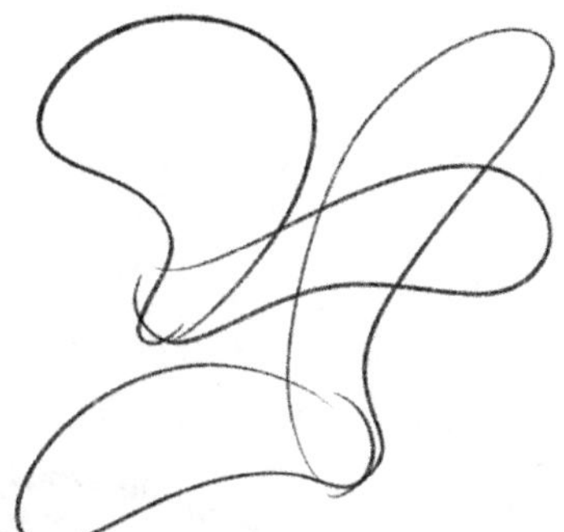

STEP 2
Last shapes and add-ons

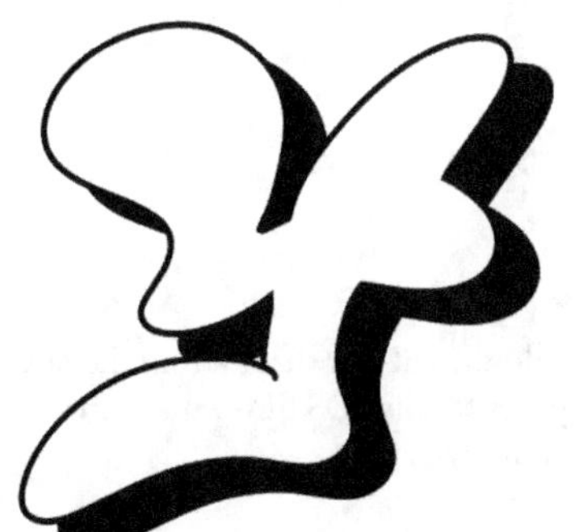

STEP 3
Outline and shadow

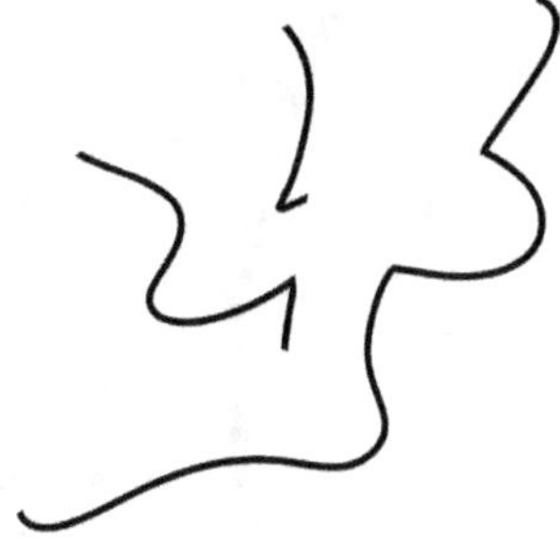

STEP 1
Finish outline

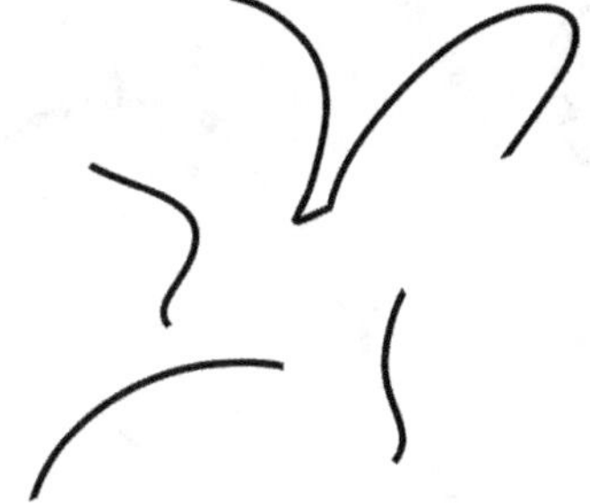

STEP 2
Finish outline and shadow

STEP 3
Do it yourself!

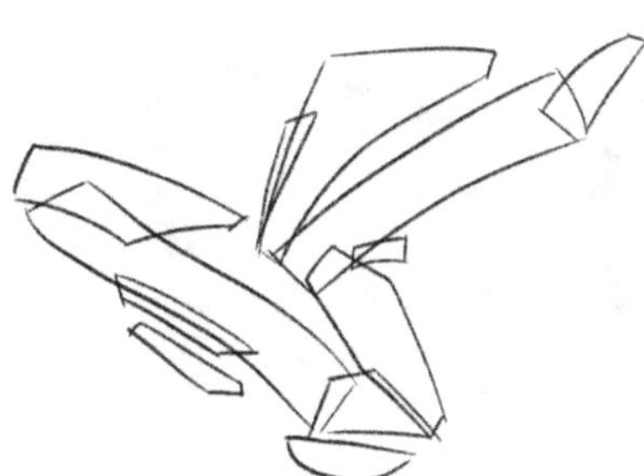

STEP 1
Basic shapes

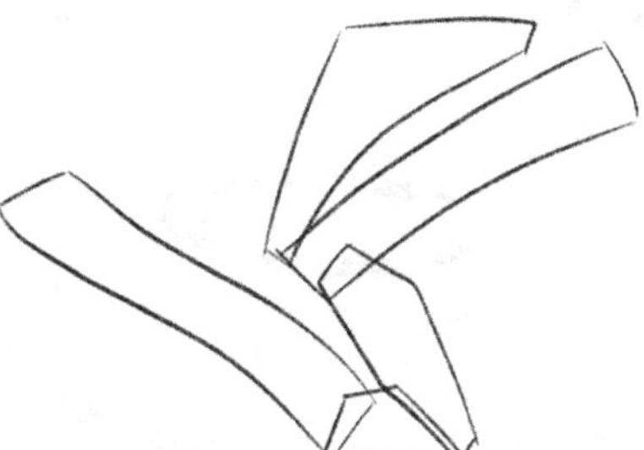

STEP 2
Last shapes and add-ons

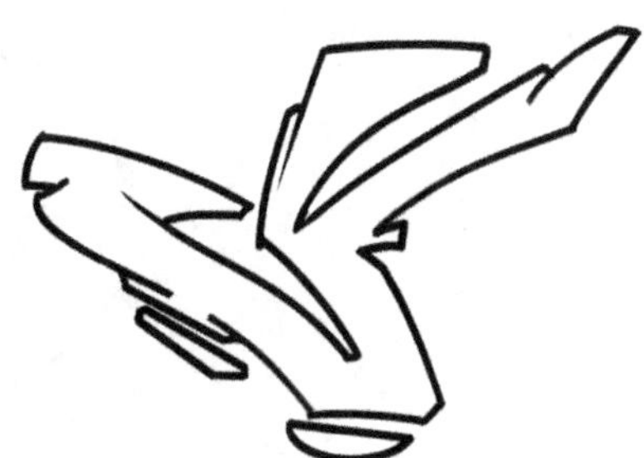

STEP 3
Outline

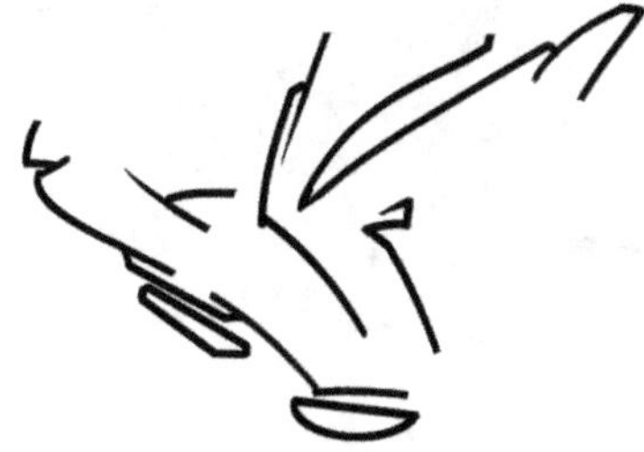

STEP 1
Finish outline

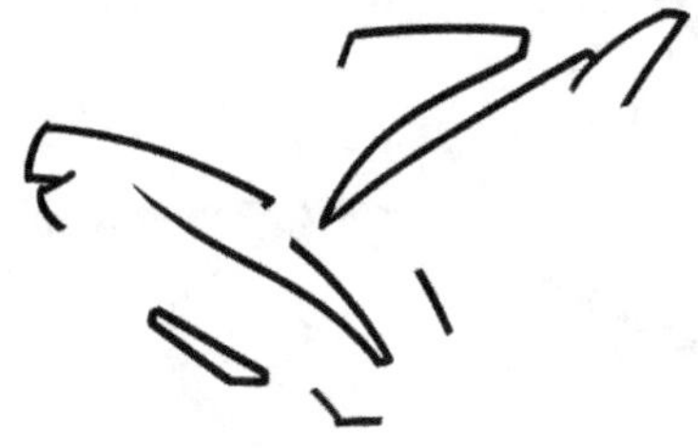

STEP 2
Finish outline

STEP 3
Do it yourself!

Add the cut-out shapes from the next
pages to this FOS throw up to create
your own style!

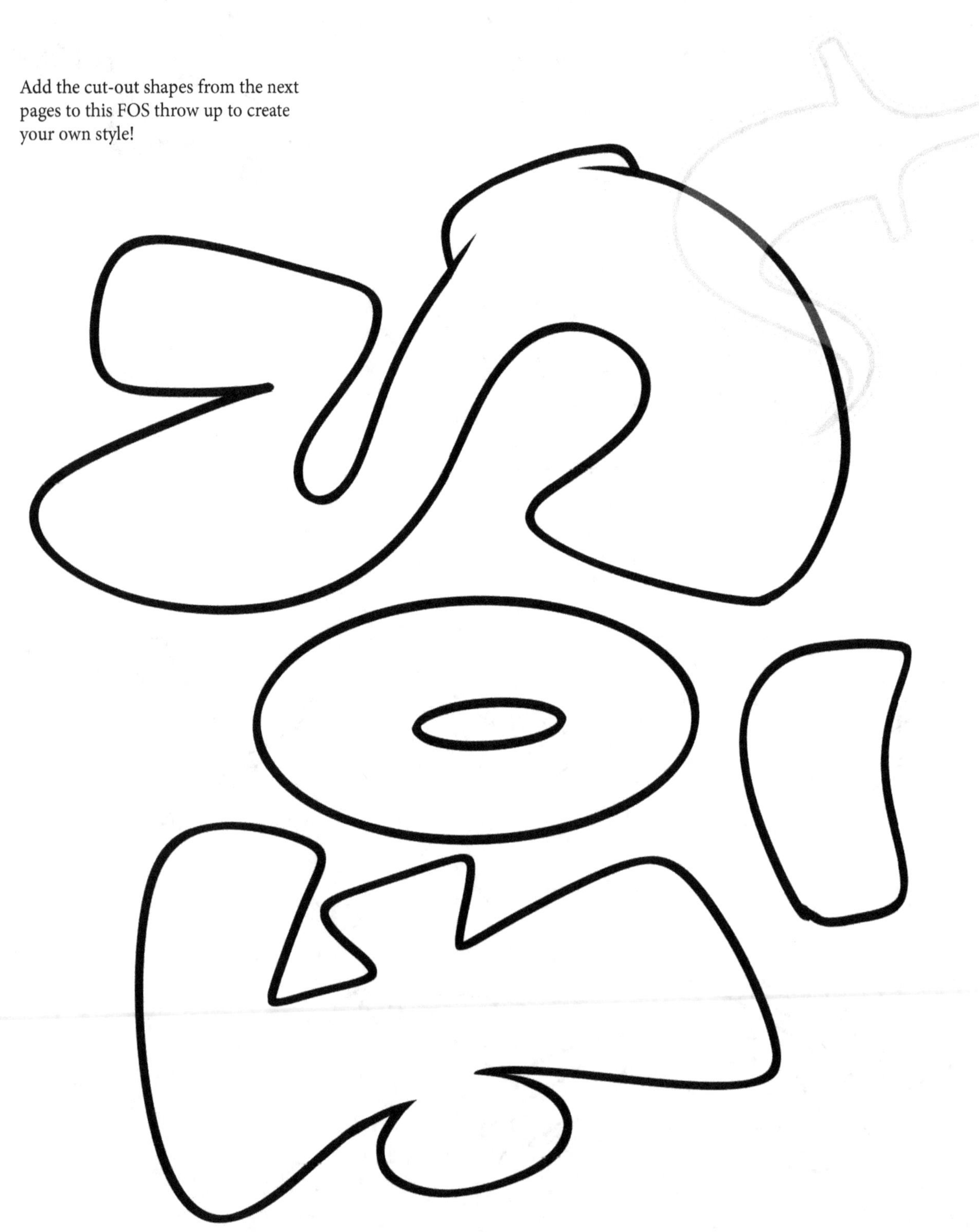

Paper Cut-out add-ons

CUT OUT THE SHAPES, AND BUILD
YOUR OWN LETTERS

The following pages contains shapes meant to be cut out directly from the book. These shapes and add-ons are made with the same overall style so it's easy for you to combine into your own new graffiti letters and pieces!

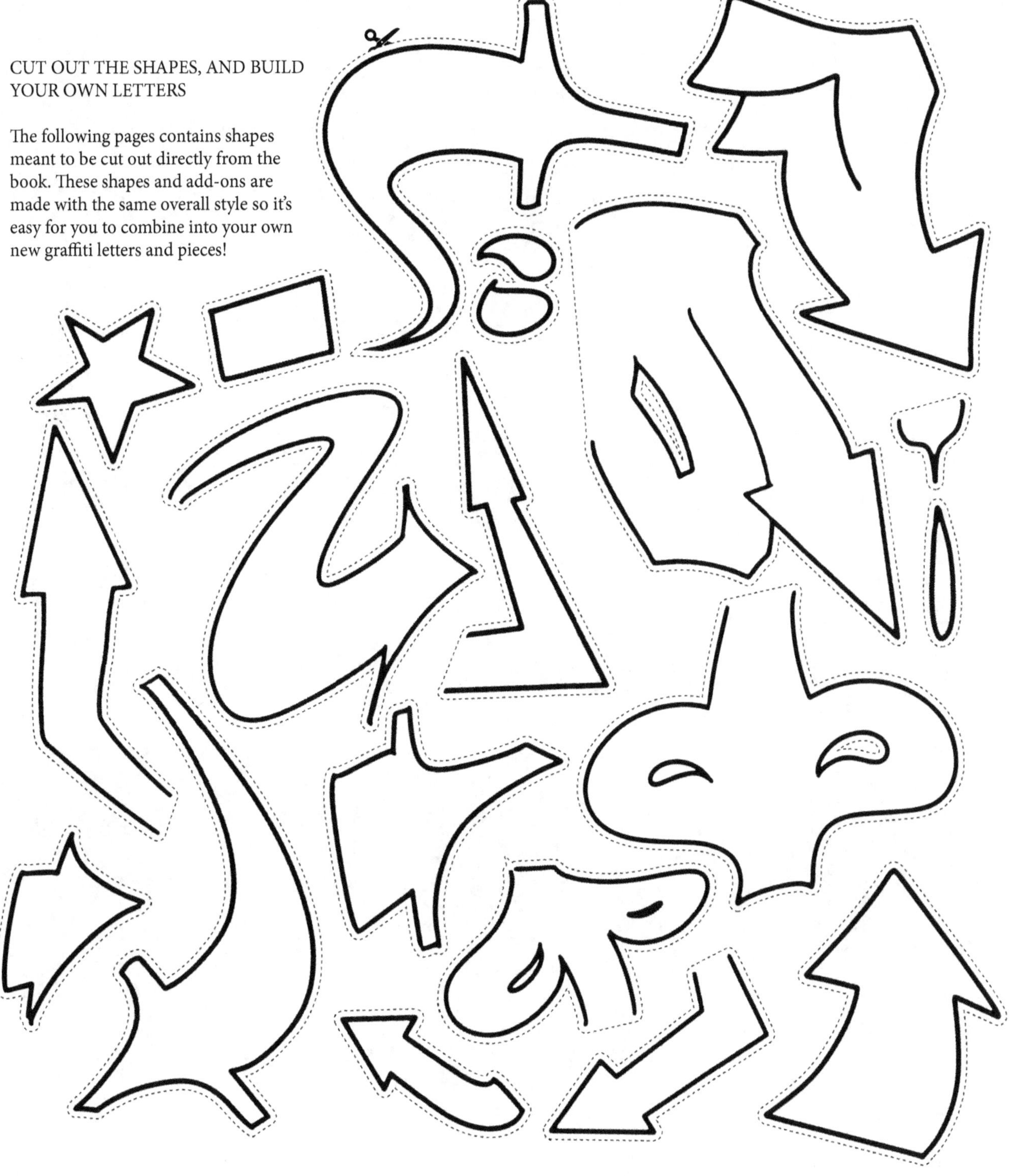

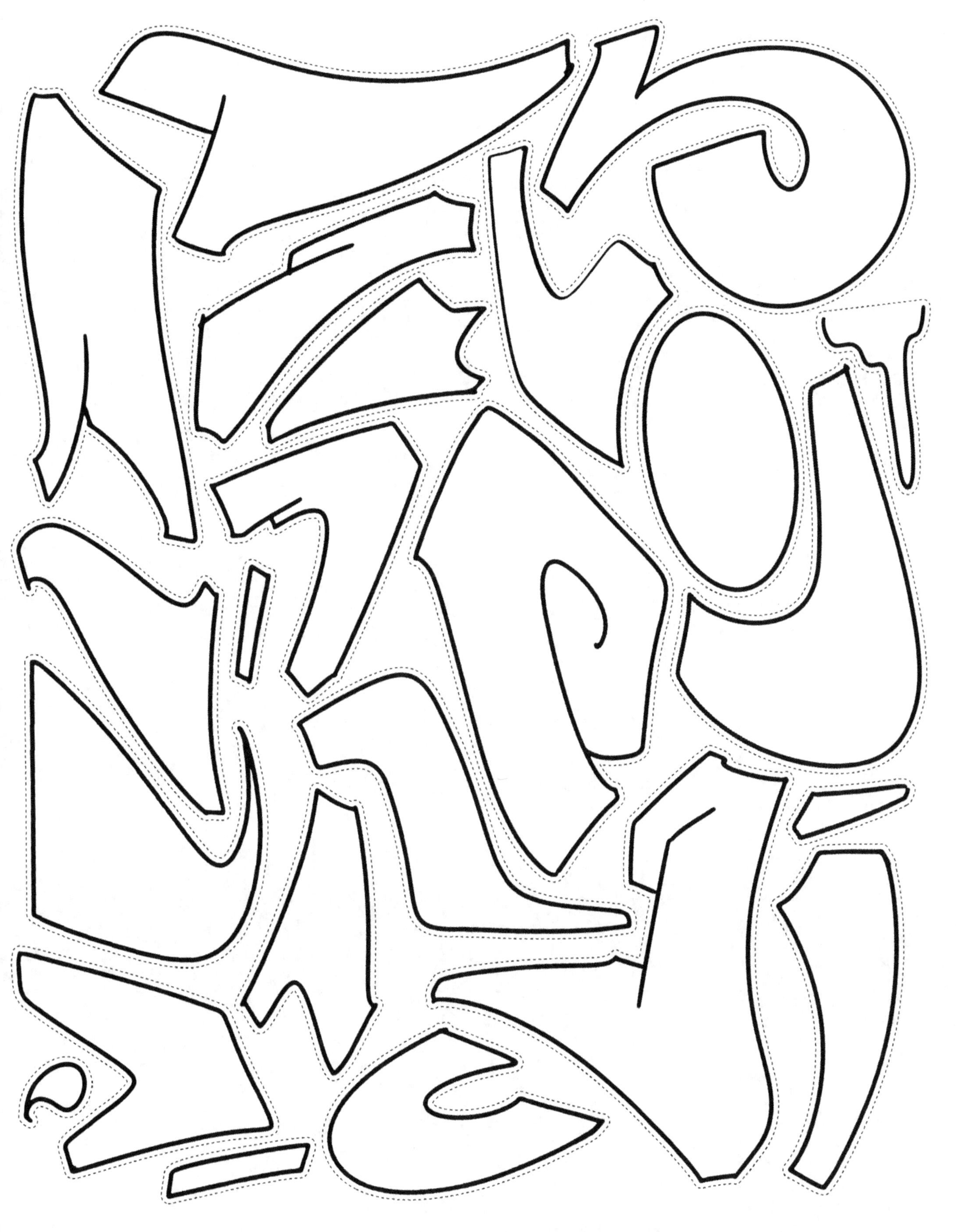

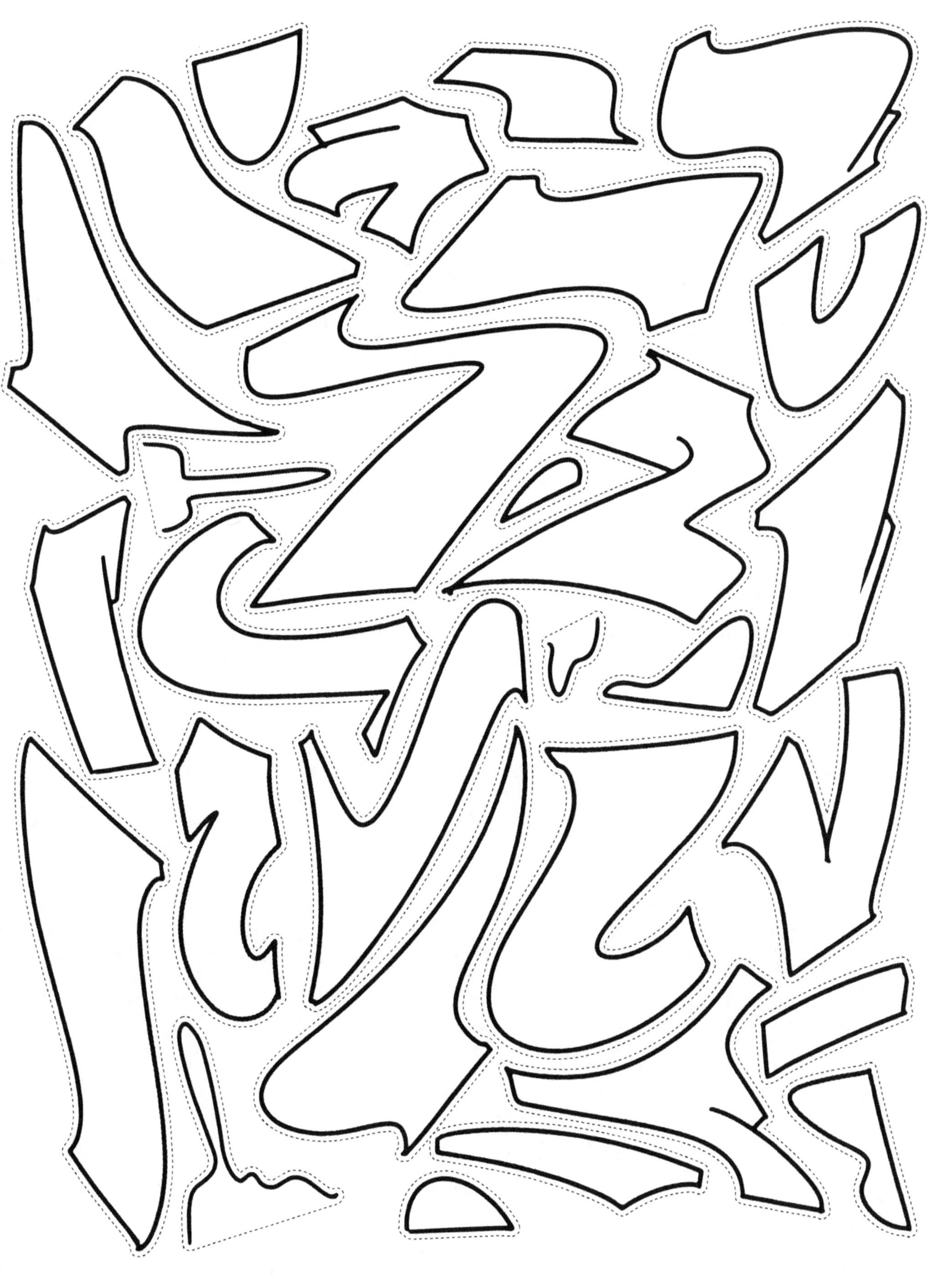

Need more inspiration?

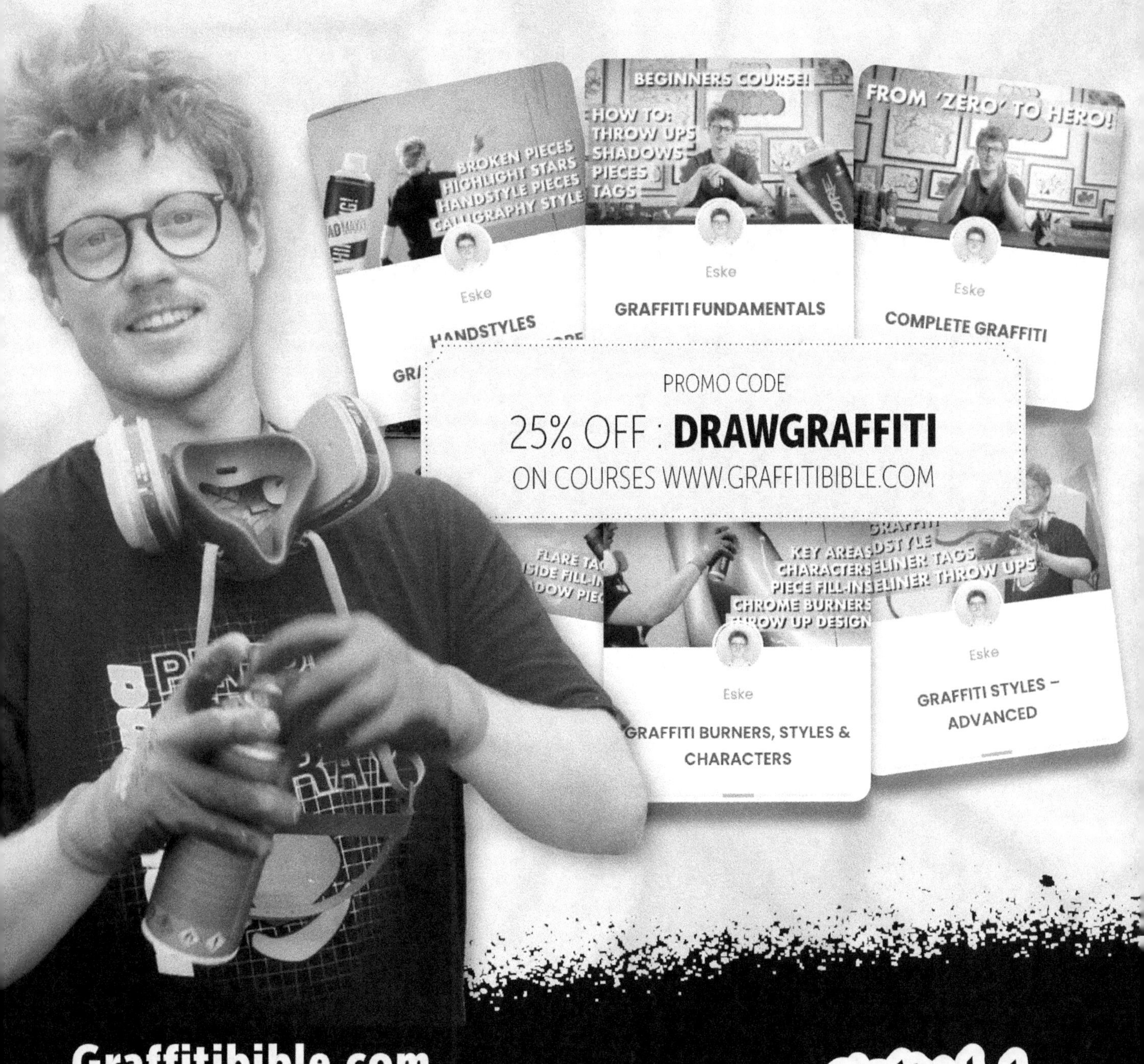

Graffitibible.com

Deepen your knowledge and create arsenal, visit our online platform

| Indepth video courses with instructor | Procreate Brush Packs |
| Free Tutorials | Inspiration and interviews from famous writers |

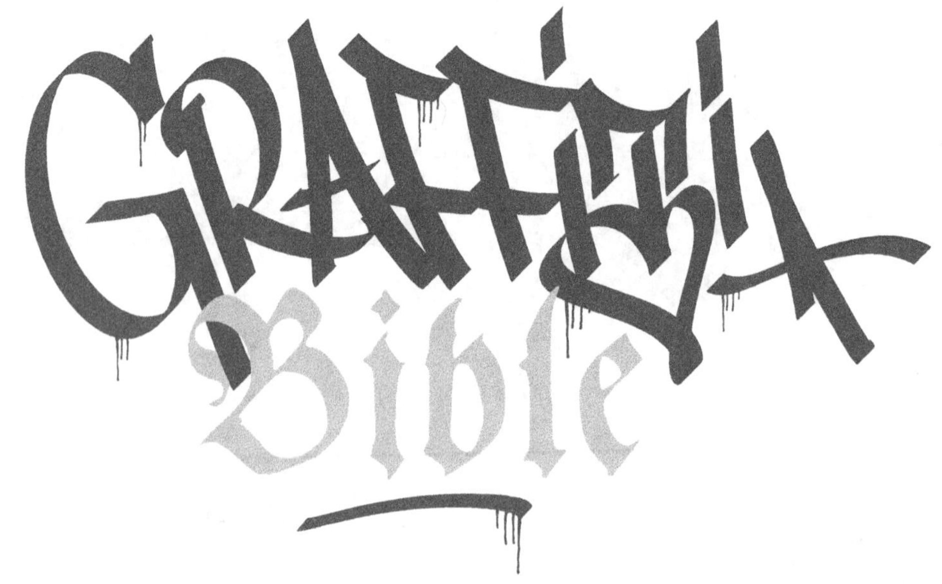